# IT'S
# 5 O'CLOCK

# The Hour of Great Grace

# And

# Collecting of the Spoils

Apostle Winston G. Baker

IT'S 5 O'CLOCK
The Hour of Great Grace and Collecting of the Spoils
Copyright ©2025 Winston G. Baker

9781506914640 PBK
9781506914657 EBK

April 2025

Published and Distributed by
First Edition Design Publishing, Inc.
P.O. Box 17646, Sarasota, FL 34276-3217
www.firsteditiondesignpublishing.com

All scriptures quoted are from the King James Version of the Holy Bible.

*And when Jehoshaphat and his people came to take away the spoil of them, they found among them in abundance both riches with the dead bodies, and precious jewels, which they stripped off for themselves, more than they could carry away: and they were three days in gathering of the spoil, it was so much.* 2 Chronicles 20:25

You are at the right place, at the right time, for your miracle.

You are at the right place, at the right time, for your breakthrough.

# Table of Contents

# Introduction

God says to tell you - "It's five o'clock - the hour of great grace!"

Five o'clock is the final hour in the final watch of the day. The Bible mentions different watches, which carry deep physical and spiritual meanings.

The night is divided into four watches with three hours in each watch as shown below:

6 p.m. to 9 p.m. or the "evening watch" is the first watch of the night.

9 p.m. to 12 midnight is the midnight watch and is the second watch of the night.

12 midnight to 3 a.m. is the "Cock-crowing" watch and is the third watch of the night.

3 a.m. to 6 a.m. is the "morning watch" and is the fourth watch of the night.

Then comes daybreak!

This is the moment of light - daylight - the commencement of man's labour.

The first hour of the day begins at 6 a.m.

The first watch of the day is 6 a.m. to 9 a.m.

The second watch of the day is 9 a.m. to 12 noon.

The third watch of the day is 12 noon to 3 p.m.

The fourth and final watch of the day is 3 p.m. to 6 p.m.

The final hour in the final watch of the day is 5 p.m. to 6 p.m.

So 5 p.m. is the 11th and final hour of the day. This hour is of great significance, both physically and spiritually.

I intend to heighten your awareness that this is the hour in which we are living, and it is a crucial moment in the life of the church.

Under the unction of the Holy Spirit, I release this powerful truth for believers in the year Two Thousand and Twenty-five and beyond. He that hath an ear to hear, let him hear what the Spirit of God is saying to the churches. "It's high time to awake!" says the Lord. "Awake out of your slumber! Awake out of your sleep! Be sober and be vigilant!"

It's time to reap the end-time harvest. Truly, the harvest is ripe, but the labourers are few. I pray earnestly that the Lord of the harvest will send forth labourers into His vineyard.

I also pray for comprehensive blood coverage over every reader and listener. I am all too aware of the enemy's onslaught each time I obey the unction of the Holy Spirit to release a prophetic word.

The reason for the attacks on readers and listeners is the fact that eyes and ears are being opened as you read and listen. The devil knows how powerful this knowledge is and that it brings deliverance to those who are bound, but I cover you in the name of Jesus Christ of Nazareth.

## Prayer

**Father, in the name of Jesus Christ,**
**I thank You for every reader and listener.**
**I thank You for another opportunity to be Your finger, writing on the hearts of Your precious people.**
**As they engage in the search for knowledge and truth;**
**Lord, please increase their understanding and grant them the necessary wisdom to apply the truths they unearth.**
**I pray that great grace will be poured upon everyone who receives this word.**
**I come against every attack.**
**I come against every backlash.**
**I come against untimely death.**
**I come against violence.**
**I come against murder.**
**I come against the onslaught of devouring spirits.**
**I wage war against every spirit that undermines.**

I declare and decree that Your people shall go forward in great grace in Two Thousand and Twenty-Five and beyond.

I decree and declare that they will collect the spoils of the enemy, as You fight their battles and give them victory,

I give You thanks.

I give You all the glory.

I give You all the praise,

In Jesus' mighty name.

Amen.

# Chapter 1

# Timing is Everything

The Spirit of God pulled me into His belly during the final days of Two Thousand and Twenty-Four. He said, "Son, the ministry I have given you is global because you obey My voice when I speak to you. The year into which you are crossing over is the year of five." He said, "Do not focus on rhymes; I want you to be focused on rhythms. I want you to focus on what is divine; I want you to focus on the time."

He further said, "I need a voice that will speak 'Thus saith God' regardless of what other voices are saying. You don't need to be loud, but you need to be profound. You need to listen and speak at My unction. Don't focus on the crowd. I have already told you that greatness is invisible, but its presence can be felt – yes, greatness is tangible."

The Lord reminded me that He is doing a quick work and that we should redeem the time because the days are evil. He reminded me of 'time'. He impressed on me the urgency to release this word because it is time for a quantum leap in the King Jesus Pentecostal Fellowship and the body of Christ globally. This is a compass to help provide guidance as we navigate the challenges of the year 2025 and new seasons in general.

Herein lies information and revelations to increase our knowledge of who we are, where we are coming from, where we are going, and how to get there.

More importantly, we will discover what time it is in our lives. What time it is in earth, as well as the spiritual realm. There will emerge a heightened awareness of what we are to be doing in this hour.

In the process of preparation, I have been reminded of my mandate, given to me over twenty years ago when I encountered Jesus Christ who became my Lord and Saviour. The only true and living God, who was and is and is to come. The only potentate. The only wise God, ever living, ever faithful; His name is Jesus.

I serve no other god but Jesus Christ. My Creator, Redeemer, Provider, Protector, Sustainer, Peace, Comforter, Salvation, and soon coming King. Glory be to the Most High God! Glory, honour, and praises be unto Him forever, Amen.

In the first chapter of the Bible -the book of beginnings, called Genesis- God carefully laid the foundation of the earth and the order of things. We refer to it as the creation story. The first five verses go like this:

1. In the beginning God created the heaven and the earth.
2. And the earth was without form, and void; and darkness was upon the face of the deep. And the Spirit of God moved upon the face of the waters.

3.  And God said, Let there be light: and there was light.

4.  And God saw the light, that it was good: and God divided the light from the darkness.

5.  And God called the light Day, and the darkness He called Night. And the evening and the morning were the first day.

Etched in these first five verses of the Torah or Pentateuch is the story of how time began. Of note in verse five, the Bible did not say that the morning and the evening were the first day. Instead, it says that the evening and the morning were the first day.

This declaration is powerful and revelatory. God is from everlasting to everlasting, but in His masterplan was the creation of the earth. At this juncture, He stepped out of eternity and established time.

God drew two lines in eternity; one marks the beginning of time and the other marks the end of time on earth. Spirit beings dwell in eternity and can only operate legally in earth with a physical body. So, God created human beings with mortal bodies to exist in time. Each man makes two marks on this timeline. One marks our entrance into this world at birth and the other marks our exit at death.

The space between these two marks in time is called 'our time on earth' or 'our lifetime'. This time is divided into years, months, weeks, days, hours, minutes, and seconds. Each of us is placed in earth for a set time.

After this, we will meet our Creator at the judgment to give an account of our deeds in time.

A visit to the cemetery reveals the time those who are buried there spent on earth. The date of their entry is followed by a dash (-) and then the date of their departure. What is done in the dash (-) determines where they will spend eternity. If you are reading or listening to this book, it means that you are still writing your story in time, so take heed.

Time is divided into hours, minutes, and seconds. Various tools have been invented to measure time. Before the introduction of sophisticated tools, men used shadows cast by the sun, sundials, hourglass as well as the crowing of the cock to help determine the time of day.

As time progressed, several tools have been invented to measure time with accuracy and precision. These range from the old grandfather clock to digital and analogue clocks, wrist-watches, stop-watches, atomic clocks and chronometers.

Another important time tool is the calendar. This is used to measure days, weeks, months and years. Early calendars include the Sumerian, Egyptian and Babylonian calendars.

Later, the Hellenic and Julian calendars were developed. The latter was introduced by Julius Caesar in 46 BC, with an extra day added to the month of February every four years. This is known as a Leap Year.

Pope Gregory XIII released a refinement of the Julian Calendar in 1582. It is known as the Gregorian Calendar and is currently used worldwide.

This brief walk through the history of time was a deliberate effort to establish the framework for the rest of my discourse. Marcus Garvey once said, "A people without knowledge of their past history, origin, and culture is like a tree without roots."

The Lord said in **Hosea 4:6** - *My people are destroyed for lack of knowledge…*

This cannot be truer when it comes to the matter of 'time'. Many believe that there is an error in Genesis 1:5 when it is compared with modern information on time.

I repeat the verse here for emphasis:

*And God called the light Day, and the darkness He called Night. And the evening and the morning were the first day.*

Man has changed what God established in the beginning and now teaches that a day begins and ends at midnight. However, a closer look at the scripture not only reveals the truth but also the power of God.

God's omnipotence, omniscience, and omnipresence are quite evident in the exploration of His word concerning time. Additionally, it reveals the nature and characteristics of God.

The evening being mentioned before the morning was intentional. It is a declaration of the fact that God knows the end from the beginning. It shows us that He writes the end of the script and then places us at the beginning to walk to the end of time.

Have you noticed how time begins with the darkness of evening and ends with the light of day? God created all things and established earth's modus operandi. He then created His Masterpiece -man- and gave him the day to work and the night to rest.

Watch this! While the flesh man works in the day, the spirit man is quiet. However, when night comes and the physical man is tired and goes to rest, the spirit man comes alive. The scripture tells us that a lot of activities take place during this time, especially in the spirit realm.

This explains why it is so important for us to obey the nudging of the Spirit of God during the night watches to pray. Whenever the Spirit of God wakes us up at any watch of the night, we should get up and pray.

Thanks be to God! He works the night shift! Once we have obeyed His voice and prayed, like David, we can go to our beds and sleep. David boasts in

**Psalm 4:8 -** *I will both lay me down in peace, and sleep: for Thou Lord, only makest me dwell in safety.*

God's pattern in creation was also revelatory.

**Matthew 20:16** says- *So the last shall be first, and the first last. We expect evening to be last,*

10

but God puts evening first. Likewise, we expect morning to be first, but God puts morning last.

From Genesis to Revelation, we see this declaration unfolding. It began with the first and the last Adam. What the first Adam was supposed to give us, he allowed the enemy to steal when he transgressed. But thanks be to God, the last Adam came and retrieved it. Through His redemptive work, He took it back from the enemy and made it available to us again.

The birthright or father's greatest blessing, rightly belongs to the first-born son. However, several times in scripture, we see God giving the birthright to the last son instead of the firstborn. It happened with Esau and Jacob. It happened with Ephraim and Manasseh and is currently happening with the Jews and Gentiles.

God told me to tell you that He is about to do it again in the year 2025. This time, it's going to happen to you. However, He says conditions apply.

Like the sons of Issachar, you must be able to discern times and seasons. It's imperative to be knowledgeable of God's timing and to understand what we are required to do in each season.

Timing is everything!

The pattern of things established by mankind over the years sometimes blurs our vision of what God is doing in the realm of the spirit. This inability to perceive the move of God can be detrimental to the destiny of an individual.

Being housed in this human body, we sometimes forget that we are spirit beings having an earthly experience. These man-made calendars and teachings concerning time, often shift our focus from God's mandate for us to our fleshly desires and dictates.

God said, in **Genesis 1:14 -** *Let there be lights in the firmament of the heaven to divide the day from the night; and let them be for signs, and for seasons, and for days, and years.*

In the latter part of the book of Genesis, the sons of Issachar came to prominence.

**1 Chronicles 12:32** says this of them: *And of the children of Issachar, which were men that had understanding of the times to know what Israel ought to do; the heads of them were two hundred, and all their brethren were at their commandment.*

Beware! Now is not the time to be distracted. Time is coming to a close! The end of time is upon us; eternity is drawing near. Look out! Paul, in **Ephesians 5:15-17** admonished us:

*See then that ye walk circumspectly, not as fools, but as wise,*
    *redeeming the time, because the days are evil.*
    *Wherefore be ye not unwise, but understanding what the will of the Lord is.*

Harvest time is near!

## Matthew 13:24-30

*24 Another parable put He forth unto them, saying, The kingdom of heaven is likened unto a man which sowed good seed in his field.*

*25 But while men slept, his enemy came and sowed tares among the wheat, and went his way.*

*26 But when the blade was sprung up, and brought forth fruit, then appeared the tares also.*

*27 So the servants of the householder came and said unto him, Sir, didst not thou sow good seed in thy field? From whence then hath it tares?*

*28 He said unto them, An enemy hath done this. The servants said unto him, Wilt thou then that we go and gather them up?*

*29 But he said, Nay; lest while ye gather up the tares, ye root up also the wheat with them.*

*30 Let both grow together until the harvest: and in the time of harvest I will say to the reapers, Gather ye together first the tares, and bind them in bundles to burn them: but gather the wheat into my barn.*

Timing is everything. The Bible says there is a time to everything. There is a season and a time for every purpose under heaven. A time to plant and a time to pluck up that which is planted.

Do you know the difference in your life? The difference between when to plant and when to pluck up? Have you ever asked God to pluck up what He did not plant, even if you have got accustomed to it? Or do you intend to keep it at all costs?

The reality is that you can't have a new season until you are willing to say goodbye to the current season. I call it 'The Art of Letting Go'. It's the spirit of release; not wrestling but releasing. Some of you are wrestling to keep that which you should release.

Here is a word of wisdom to anyone holding on to something that God is trying to take away from you. Right now, you need to release it -simply let it go. That was for that season! Holding on to what needs to be let go of is delaying you from receiving the blessings God has for you in this season.

### Ecclesiastes 3:1-8

*1 To everything there is a season, and a time to every purpose under the heaven.*

*2 A time to be born, and a time to die; a time to plant, and a time to pluck up that which is planted;*

*3 A time to kill, and a time to heal; a time to break down and a time to build up;*

*4 A time to weep, and a time to laugh; a time to mourn, and a time to dance;*

*5 A time to cast away stones, and a time to gather stones together; a time to embrace, and a time to refrain from embracing;*

*6 A time to get, and a time to lose; a time to keep, and a time to cast away;*

*7 A time to rend, and a time to sew; a time to keep silence, and a time to speak;*

*8 A time to love, and a time to hate; a time of war, and a time of peace.*

Everything about life is timing. Those who play football and enjoy juggling the ball like I do know that when you juggle, you must juggle with timing.

If cricket is your favourite game, you know that whenever you arc holding the bat and someone is bowling, you must have good timing to hit the ball. You can't swing the bat too early, neither can you swing it too late. The bat must be swung at the correct time.

In a track and field race, a false start occurs when a competitor leaves the block before the official signals the athletes to begin the race. A false start means that the athlete has missed the timing. This immediately disqualifies the individual from the race.

Timing is not only important in sports. It is equally, and some might argue, more important when you speak. Timing is important in sharing a joke. It's not just about whether you can tell a good joke or not. It's also about the timing of the joke.

The right joke at the wrong time can lead to violence and even death. You might have heard the Jamaican proverb, 'Frog seh, wat is joke to yuh, a death to mi'. This means that we must not only pay attention to what is being said, but also to when it is being said. What you joked about at the wrong time can be insensitive and damaging to someone else.

Being confident, knowledgeable, and eloquent in your delivery of a message is commendable. But the question is: Can you convey the information with proper timing? You can share valuable information at an inappropriate time. Your delivery might be impressive, but your failure to observe timing results in you being labelled an incompetent speaker.

You can be right about what you said but wrong about when you said it. Even with the best intentions, you end up doing more harm than good.

So, it's not about being right or wrong. It is about timing. The right information, delivered at the wrong time, has torn numerous families and households apart. It has reduced the feelings of kings to that of servants. Poor timing can hinder that dream house from being built. It can block you from receiving that vehicle and delay that promotion or long-awaited breakthrough.

The right information, given at the wrong time, can cost you your peace of mind. I know many of you are adamant about proving that you are right. However, you should be more concerned about what is more important; that is 'the right time'.

Timing is important in music, be it instrumentals or vocals. Sounds and beats are placed in time in the composition of music. This is called rhythm. Simply put, rhythm is the element of music that deals with the arrangement of sounds and silences in relation to time. So, to be out of rhythm is to be out of timing.

Everything is about timing. Everything has a rhythm. God has a rhythm. Breathing has a rhythm. Blood circulation has a rhythm. Pulse has a rhythm, which is evidenced by our heartbeats.

Everything alive has a rhythm. Birds have a rhythm. A woman's body has a rhythm. It is called 'her cycle'. Missing that cycle raises an alarm. It could mean that a woman has conceived or that her health is under attack.

God is repeatedly speaking in creation, nature, and procreation. His message is this: Timing is everything. Listen to me! You cannot be fruitful out of your season. Right where you are, say 'Lord, teach me to know my season!' Ask Him to help you with your timing. Time! Time! Time! Timing is everything. There are a few things that I am sure of in my life and ministry. The motto of King Jesus Pentecostal Fellowship is one such.

It says:

*You are at the right place, at the right time for your miracle.*

*You are at the right place, at the right time for your breakthrough.*

It was the right time when God sent me to 138-140 Red Hills Road, Kingston – the present location of the ministry's headquarters. It was not just the right time in my life, it was the right time in Kingston. It was the right time in history.

To be effective, things must be done at the right time. Let me reiterate - you must understand timing. By now, this phrase sounds redundant, but I am going to repeat it. Timing is everything!

What is timing? Timing is everything! God sent me to ask you, 'Do you know what time it is in your life?' I wear a watch, and I have a mobile phone. This keeps me abreast of the time of day. However, what is crucial is to know what time it is in my life. Where am I on my timeline in earth?

David was cognizant of this.

He prayed in **Psalm 90:12,** *So teach us to number our days, that we may apply our hearts unto wisdom.*

Do you know what time it is in your life? Is it time to pluck up? Is it time to put away childish things? According to the Bible, you shall be fruitful in your season. Your leaves shall not wither, and whatsoever you do shall prosper in your season.

If I can only be fruitful in my season, it follows that I need to be aware of my season to be fruitful. You've got to know when to hold it and when to fold it. Contrary to what many believe, folding at the right time is not a failure.

It's all about timing! In Genesis 1:14, the Bible speaks of the lights created for day, night, years, signs and seasons. This reveals that there are various dimensions of light. The sons of Issachar were gifted with knowledge of these dimensions.

Issachar is the ninth son of Jacob and the fifth son of Leah. The Bible lets us know that the sons of Issachar had understanding. Not just of things, but also of time. This enabled them to know what Israel needed to do and more importantly, when to do what.

Understanding time and knowing when to do what are abilities that I call 'the dynamic duo'. It catapulted the sons of Issachar to a position of authority in Israel. The Biblical Hall of Fame is decorated with people of faith who also possessed this dynamic duo.

With these abilities, lights are recognised as handwritings on the walls of time, placed there by the

Creator for information and direction. They inform us of when seasons end and when seasons begin. Additionally, there is an understanding of what is to be done in each season.

Stepping into this realm will be discussed in a subsequent chapter. It is, however, time for introspection. Turn the searchlight inwards and pray earnestly that God will reveal to you the season of life you are currently in.

Let Him instruct you as to what you ought to be doing presently. When you have heard from Him, give Him thanks and ensure that you obey those instructions.

# Chapter 2

# The First Hour of The Day

**Matthew 20:1-2**
*1 For the kingdom of heaven is like unto a man that is an householder, which went out early in the morning to hire labourers into his vineyard.*
*2 And when he had agreed with the labourers for a penny a day, he sent them into his vineyard.*

This is one of the parables of Jesus. A parable is a spiritual truth being conveyed through a physical situation. Jesus used this method to teach because He is not at the same level as we are.

When He came to earth, He said, *"The foxes have holes and birds of the air have nest; but the Son of man hath not where to lay His head."* **Matthew 8:20, Luke 9:58.**

This was Jesus' way of saying that birds, referring to demonic spirits, have others with which to associate. They come together for counsel, giving and taking advice.

Foxes here represent governments. Do you remember the content of Jesus' message to Herod in **Luke 13:32**? He said,

*"Go ye and tell that fox, Behold, I cast out devils, and I do cures today and tomorrow, and the third day I shall be perfected."*

So, like the demonic spirits, the heads of government gather and take sweet counsel together. This was quite the opposite with the Son of man when He came to earth. He could take counsel from no one. That is what Jesus meant when He said that the Son of man has nowhere to lay His head.

There was no match for Him on earth because of the dimension from which He operated. Neither was there anyone from whom He could take counsel, considering His high level of thinking and the vastness of His knowledge. For this reason, Jesus used parables as His primary means of communicating with men whilst on earth.

Under the old covenant, men were unable to handle revelations from the spirit realm. They could only see in the physical realm. Had Jesus not spoken in parables, no one would have understood His messages.

Until Jesus experienced death, resurrection and ascension to heaven, to be at the right hand of the Father, man remained spiritually dead. These were prerequisites to man receiving the Holy Ghost, which would restore to man the power to access the spirit realm.

**Matthew 9:17 says:**
*Neither do men put new wine into old bottles: else the bottles break, and the wine runneth out, and the*

***bottles perish: but they put new wine into new bottles, and both are preserved.***

So, Jesus spoke to the people in a manner that they could understand. This was with the knowledge that when the Holy Spirit came, their spiritual eyes would be opened, and they would eventually understand what He had been saying to them all along.

Nonetheless, from time to time, Jesus took the disciples apart from the crowd and explained the parables to them. Even so, they too remained in the dark about some of His teachings, until after the resurrection of Jesus and the baptism of the Holy Ghost.

In this parable, Jesus is the Master of the vineyard, which represents the world. He has been recruiting labourers for His vineyard since the beginning of His ministry on earth.

The first set of labourers were recruited early morning. This refers to daybreak or 6 a.m. At first glance, it appears as though there was nothing significant about this recruitment. However, a closer examination reveals that there is much to discover about this set.

These came early in the morning – the first hour of the day and were possibly few. These would be in the field for the entire day. Although they agreed with the master of the vineyard about the remuneration offered, they were later discontent, when others who came in at the last hour of the workday got the same amount as they received. The actions of this set of labourers are of great spiritual significance to the Church.

## THE FIRST HOUR OUTPOURING

**Matthew 10:1-8**
**King James Version**

*1And when he had called unto him his twelve disciples, he gave them power against unclean spirits, to cast them out, and to heal all manner of sickness and all manner of disease.*

*2 Now the names of the twelve apostles are these; The first, Simon, who is called Peter, and Andrew his brother; James the son of Zebedee, and John his brother;*

*3 Philip, and Bartholomew; Thomas, and Matthew the publican; James the son of Alphaeus, and Lebbaeus, whose surname was Thaddaeus;*

*4 Simon the Canaanite, and Judas Iscariot, who also betrayed him.*

*5 These twelve Jesus sent forth, and commanded them, saying, Go not into the way of the Gentiles, and into any city of the Samaritans enter ye not:*

*6 But go rather to the lost sheep of the house of Israel.*

*7 And as ye go, preach, saying, The kingdom of heaven is at hand.*

*8 Heal the sick, cleanse the lepers, raise the dead, cast out devils: freely ye have received, freely give.*

Jesus, the true Husbandman and Master of the vineyard, called twelve disciples at the beginning of His ministry. This signifies the establishment of the foundation of the Church, the ecclesia, the called-out ones.

Jesus Christ is the one true foundation. He is the Chief Cornerstone. He remains the Head of the Church and all those who enter into the vineyard are only fellow labourers and not owners in any way.

Notice that while Jesus laid the foundation, these twelve were referred to as disciples or followers of Christ. They were constantly at His feet, learning.

Even at the time noted in the aforementioned scripture when He sent them to do ministry, they had not yet received the infilling of the Holy Ghost. What He did was to place an anointing upon them to fulfil that particular assignment.

Although they later received the Holy Ghost and were used to do greater miracles, they remained cognizant of the fact that they were all labourers in the vineyard.

Paul discovered that the Corinthian labourers were disgruntled about the order of things in the vineyard, and he gave them this admonition, which we all need to bear in mind as believers.

### 1Corithians 3: 1-11.

*1 And I, brethren, could not speak unto you as unto spiritual, but as unto carnal, even as unto babes in Christ.*

*2 I have fed you with milk, and not with meat: for hitherto ye were not able to bear it, neither yet now are ye able.*

*3 For ye are yet carnal: for whereas there is among you envying, and strife, and divisions, are ye not carnal, and walk as men?*

*4 For while one saith, I am of Paul; and another, I am of Apollos; are ye not carnal?*

*5 Who then is Paul, and who is Apollos, but ministers by whom ye believed, even as the Lord gave to every man?*

*6 I have planted, Apollos watered; but God gave the increase.*

*7 So then neither is he that planteth anything, neither he that watereth; but God that giveth the increase.*

*8 Now he that planteth and he that watereth are one: and every man shall receive his own reward according to his own labour.*

*9 For we are labourers together with God: ye are God's husbandry, ye are God's building.*

*10 According to the grace of God which is given unto me, as a wise masterbuilder, I have laid the foundation, and another buildeth thereon. But let every man take heed how he buildeth thereupon.*

*11 For other foundation can no man lay than that is laid, which is Jesus Christ.*

The foundation of a building is not obvious. However, it is what determines the strength of the building. Foundation members can easily feel unrecognised and unappreciated, especially in old age. Nonetheless, in building, everything that comes afterwards could only be because of the foundation.

Regardless of the time we enter the vineyard, everyone shall be rewarded. So, this should motivate us to strive to maintain a good attitude. Do not get jealous because it appears as though God is using others in a mightier way than He uses you. Neither should you covet those who appear to be more blessed than you are.

We are labourers together in God's vineyard.

# Chapter 3

# The Third Hour of The Day

**Matthew 20:3-4**
*3 And he went out about the third hour, and saw others standing idle in the marketplace,*
*4 And said unto them; Go ye also into the vineyard, and whatsoever is right I will give you. And they went their way.*

The second set of workers were hired at the third hour of the day, which we understand is 9 a.m. This remains a common principle in the world of work even today. We often refer to our job as our nine-to-five.

It is noteworthy that those who went into the vineyard at 6 a.m. would be working all twelve hours of the day. Those who went at 9 a.m. would work for nine hours. However, they both would experience the heat of the midday sun. If it rained, they would possibly get wet. They would most definitely get hungry, thirsty, and tired from the lengthy work hours.

The Master of the vineyard was wise. He ensured that a legal agreement or contract between Himself and his employees was in place. This included who they were working for, exactly where they would be working, their job descriptions, their work hours and the amount of remuneration or pay they would receive at the end of the workday. To this, they all agreed and went to work.

The occurrence at this time of the day, carries deep spiritual truths and revelations to be unearthed from this aspect of the parable.

## THE THIRD HOUR OUTPOURING

### Acts 2:1-15

*1 And when the day of Pentecost was fully come, they were all with one accord in one place.*

*2 And suddenly there came a sound from heaven as of a rushing mighty wind, and it filled all the house where they were sitting.*

*3 And there appeared unto them cloven tongues like as of fire, and it sat upon each of them.*

*4 And they were all filled with the Holy Ghost, and began to speak with other tongues, as the Spirit gave them utterance.*

*5And there were dwelling at Jerusalem Jews, devout men, out of every nation under heaven.*

*6 Now when this was noised abroad, the multitude came together, and were confounded, because that every man heard them speak in his own language.*

*7And they were all amazed and marvelled, saying one to another, Behold, are not all these which speak Galilaeans?*

*8 And how hear we every man in our own tongue, wherein we were born?*

*9 Parthians, and Medes, and Elamites, and the dwellers in Mesopotamia, and in Judaea, and Cappadocia, in Pontus, and Asia,*

*10 Phrygia, and Pamphylia, in Egypt, and in the parts of Libya about Cyrene, and strangers of Rome, Jews and proselytes,*

*11 Cretes and Arabians, we do hear them speak in our tongues the wonderful works of God.*

*12 And they were all amazed, and were in doubt, saying one to another, What meaneth this?*

*13 Others mocking said, These men are full of new wine.*

*14 But Peter, standing up with the eleven, lifted up his voice, and said unto them, Ye men of Judaea, and all ye that dwell at Jerusalem, be this known unto you, and hearken to my words:*

*15 For these are not drunken, as ye suppose, seeing it is but the third hour of the day.*

As mentioned earlier, labourers were recruited into a physical vineyard at the third hour of the day, which is 9 a.m. Now, in Acts Chapter Two, the dynamics shift to a spiritual recruitment. What took place at the third hour of the day or 9 a.m. here?

It was the giving or outpouring of the Holy Ghost. Jesus poured out His Spirit upon one hundred and twenty believers who were tarrying or waiting in the Upper Room. This encounter reaped an initial harvest of three thousand souls.

Peter said to the men who were mocking the move of God, *"For these are not drunken, as ye suppose, seeing it is but the third hour of the day."* In other words, it's just nine o'clock in the morning.

What am I trying to say here? When Jesus spoke in parables about hiring a set of workers at the third hour of the day, it had spiritual symbolism. It was symbolic of the outpouring of the Holy Spirit at that same hour of the day.

Notice that in the same way these labourers began reaping the physical harvest, those on whom the Holy Ghost fell began reaping the spiritual harvest of souls. Let's look at what these third-hour labourers began to do after receiving the Holy Ghost.

**Acts 2:14, 36, 37**
*14 But Peter, standing up with the eleven, lifted up his voice, and said unto them, Ye men of Judea, and all ye that dwell at Jerusalem, be this known unto you, and hearken to my words.*

*36 Therefore let all the house of Israel know assuredly, that God hath made that same Jesus, whom ye have crucified, both Lord and Christ.*

*37 Now when they heard this, they were pricked in their heart, and said unto Peter and to the rest of the apostles, Men and brethren, what shall we do?*

Peter preached the Kingdom of God unto all in his hearing and explained the mystery of Jesus Christ. He did so with the full support of the other apostles. Many were convicted and converted. They then enquired of the apostles what they needed to do.

In **Acts 2:38**, they were given these instructions:

*Repent, and be baptized everyone of you in the name of Jesus Christ for the remission of sins, and ye shall receive the gift of the Holy Ghost.*

According to scriptures, they that gladly received the word were baptized: and the same day - the third hour reapers, harvested about three thousand souls. These continued in the apostles' doctrine and fellowship, breaking of bread, praying and praising God.

Interestingly, we note also that fear came upon every soul; and many wonders and signs were done by the apostles. This symbolised the beginning of the Church Age and the Apostolic movement. It all began with a great revival!

Out of this charismatic episode, a new culture or way of life emerged among the believers. **Acts 2:44-47** states that all that believed:

1. WERE TOGETHER
2. HAD ALL THINGS COMMON
3. SOLD THEIR POSSESSIONS AND GOODS
4. PARTED THEM TO ALL MEN, AS EVERY MAN HAD NEED
5. CONTINUED DAILY WITH ONE ACCORD IN THE TEMPLE
6. BROKE BREAD FROM HOUSE TO HOUSE
7. ATE THEIR MEAT WITH GLADNESS AND SINGLENESS OF HEART

8. WERE PRAISING GOD
9. HAD FAVOUR WITH ALL THE PEOPLE.

This was the mode of operation of the third-hour labourers. And notice that God was very much at work among them. While they did their part, God did His. He confirmed their words with miracles, signs and wonders, and He added to the church daily, such as should be saved.

# Chapter 4

# The Sixth Hour of The Day

**Matthew 20: 5** *Again he went out about the sixth and ninth hour, and did likewise.*

Understandably, this parable is set in the Jewish culture. History would have us know that planting and reaping seasons were very important to them since agriculture was their main source of livelihood.

There were natural occurrences dictated by prevailing weather conditions in each season. This informed the master of the vineyard when to plant, which in turn determined when it would be harvest time. Both had serious implications on whether the master of the vineyard would have a bumper crop or a poor harvest.

Contrary to what many believe, harvest time is a time of intense labour. Jesus gave command to put in the sickle and reap, because it's harvest time. This message referred to the spiritual harvest. However, it is a labour-intense activity also.

In the church, when we talk about harvest time, many believe that this is a time when things just fall into our hands. There is a misconstrued notion that we have nothing to do at all, at all, at all. But this could not be farther from the truth.

We read of men tearing down barns and building bigger ones during the physical harvest time. Similarly, as we reap the spiritual harvest, believers should be engaged in kingdom-building activities. We should not sit idly in our ceiled houses while the house of God lies waste.

The sixth-hour labourers were employed at noon. This is an indication that the master of the vineyard was indeed a shrewd businessman. By noon, the sun would be at its peak. Most likely, the early morning and 9 a.m. labourers would be experiencing hunger and some amount of exhaustion from the heat of the midday sun.

The master of the vineyard reassessed his harvesting programme. He meticulously calculated the remaining portion of the crop to be harvested and compared it with the remaining number of work hours in the day. Realizing that he now had only six hours left, he went back to the bargaining table.

A third labourer recruitment drive was carried out, and a third set of labourers was employed at midday. Once again, as wisdom dictated, He prepared an agreement to which they consented and began working.

Watch this! While those who started working at six and nine a.m. were exhausted and needed to take a lunch break, the midday recruits were full of energy, vim, vigour and vitality. As expected, the new sixth-hour labourers began to work with fervour.

As with the first and third hour, this physical harvest experience at the sixth hour also has spiritual symbolism to the sixth hour harvest of souls.

## THE SIXTH HOUR OUTPOURING

**John 4: 5-24**

*5 Then cometh He to a city of Samaria, which is called Sychar, near to the parcel of ground that Jacob gave to his son Joseph.*

*6 Now Jacob's well was there. Jesus therefore, being wearied with His journey, sat thus on the well: and it was about the sixth hour.*

*7 There cometh a woman of Samaria to draw water: Jesus saith unto her, Give me to drink.*

*8 (For His disciples were gone away unto the city to buy meat.)*

*9 Then saith the woman of Samaria unto Him, How is it that Thou, being a Jew, askest drink of me, which am a woman of Samaria? for the Jews have no dealings with the Samaritans.*

*10 Jesus answered and said unto her, If thou knewest the gift of God, and who it is that saith to thee, Give me to drink; thou wouldest have asked of Him, and He would have given thee living water.*

*11 The woman saith unto Him, Sir, Thou hast nothing to draw with, and the well is deep: from whence then hast Thou that living water?*

*12 Art Thou greater than our father Jacob, which gave us the well, and drank thereof himself, and his children, and his cattle?*

*13 Jesus answered and said unto her, Whosoever drinketh of this water shall thirst again:*

*14 But whosoever drinketh of the water that I shall give him shall never thirst; but the water that I shall give him shall be in him a well of water springing up into everlasting life.*

*15 The woman saith unto Him, Sir, give me this water, that I thirst not, neither come hither to draw.*

*16 Jesus saith unto her, Go, call thy husband, and come hither.*

*17 The woman answered and said, I have no husband. Jesus said unto her, Thou hast well said, I have no husband:*

*18 For thou hast had five husbands; and he whom thou now hast is not thy husband: in that saidst thou truly.*

*19 The woman saith unto Him, Sir, I perceive that Thou art a prophet.*

*20 Our fathers worshipped in this mountain; and Ye say, that in Jerusalem is the place where men ought to worship.*

*21 Jesus saith unto her, Woman, believe me, the hour cometh, when ye shall neither in this mountain, nor yet at Jerusalem, worship the Father.*

*22 Ye worship ye know not what: we know what we worship: for salvation is of the Jews.*

*23 But the hour cometh, and now is, when the true worshippers shall worship the Father in spirit and in truth: for the Father seeketh such to worship Him.*

*24 God is a Spirit: and they that worship Him must worship Him in spirit and in truth.*

This woman sat at Jacob's well at the sixth hour of the day, which is noon. It is said to be an unusual occurrence for females to be at the well at this time. There are also numerous assumptions about her motive for being there at that time.

None of that is relevant to the life changing encounter she had with Jesus at the well. It all began when she tried to engage Jesus in a debate over the right place to worship. This came in response to Jesus requesting a drink of water from her.

He was intentional when He initiated that conversation. So, He remained focused on the mission in His deliberations with her. Jesus was a man on a mission. **John 4:4** says, *And He must needs go through Samaria.*

You will recall that at nine o'clock, the Holy Ghost was released on one hundred and twenty believers in the upper room. However, as was said, it had a far-reaching impact. Three thousand souls were initially garnered at the beginning of the first revival of the Church. Now, at noon, or the sixth hour of the day, the master hired another set of labourers in the physical. And as it was at 6 a.m. and 9 a.m., so it was at midday; something phenomenal was about to take place again in the spiritual realm.

The woman engaged Jesus in conversation or rather debate about worship. Jesus said, *"You worship, you know not what, but we the Jews know what we worship."* Jesus went on to unveil His hidden agenda by letting her know that He wanted to introduce her to real worship.

What is real worship? If you are going to worship God, you must worship Him in spirit and in truth. This revelation came at 12 o'clock in the day. So, at the sixth hour of the day, true worship was revealed.

Watch this now! Whenever there is a revelation at any one of the watches, there is a revival. These revivals produce a great harvest of souls. John 4:28 tells us that the woman left her waterpot and went into the city to introduce the Samaritans to Jesus.

Many of them believed on Jesus Christ after hearing her testimony but more believed because of Jesus' own words. Here, one of Jesus' main characteristics is visible. He is very passionate about harvesting the souls of men for the Kingdom of God.

The disciples returned and tried to force Him to eat physical meat. That was thoughtful and considerate, but it was poor timing for Jesus. He was more focused on feeding Samaria spiritual food.

This is what He told the disciples who were distracting Him from His mission:

*My meat is to do the will of Him that sent me, and to finish His work.*

What determination! He continued:

*Say not ye, There are yet four months, and then cometh harvest? Behold, I say unto you, Lift up your eyes, and look on the fields, for they are white already to harvest.*

Have you already repented of your sins and been baptized in the name of Jesus Christ? Have you received the Holy Ghost with the initial evidence of speaking in tongues? If your answer to those questions is 'Yes', then I have just one more question for you. What are you doing in the Kingdom of God?

We are all saved to serve! Are you passionate about reaping the lost at any cost? My brothers and sisters in Christ, it's time to get active. Get up! Souls are dying out of Christ daily. Did you tell anyone about Jesus today? Are you a witness?

If you have lost your zeal, I pray that it will be renewed, and you will experience a revival of the passion to reap souls for the Kingdom of God. Share the good news of salvation with a family member, a co-worker, a friend or an enemy today. Pray for a sinner, invite someone to church and most importantly, model Christ for the world to see.

Like the woman of Samaria, true worship has been revealed to you. Don't be selfish! Share it with someone else. Who knows, God might be waiting to use you to begin the next revival in your community.

# Chapter 5

# The Ninth Hour of The Day

In **Matthew 26:41**, Jesus said to Peter:

*Watch and pray, that ye enter not into temptation: the spirit indeed is willing, but the flesh is weak.*

Jesus had taken His disciples to the Mount of Olives after the last supper. There He explained to them that He was about to be crucified. He told them that they would all reject Him that night. This made them furious.

They tried desperately to reassure Him of their undying loyalty and to convince Him that He was wrong. Peter, a rock - the key man, took it personally. He said to Jesus:

*Though all men shall be offended because of Thee, yet will I never be offended.*

In response, Jesus told Peter that before the cock crowed, that same night, He would deny Him three times. Peter became even more defensive. This time, he said to Jesus:

*Though I should die with Thee, yet will I not deny Thee. Likewise said also all the disciples.*

Jesus, knowing what time it was in His life, didn't continue the conversation. Instead, He proceeded to Gethsemane. He told them to sit there while He went further to pray. Jesus took Peter and the sons of Zebedee with Him.

He was facing His most difficult time as a man. The Lord was about to be apprehended, tried, and crucified. Judas had slipped away from the company of the other disciples and was busy tracking Jesus' location.

He had agreed to betray Him to the religious leaders with a kiss for a measly thirty pieces of silver. Having already collected the money, he now had to uphold his end of the bargain. He needed to identify Jesus so that they could apprehend Him.

As the weight of the sins of man pressured Jesus, He confessed to the three disciples who were with Him:

*My soul is exceeding sorrowful, even unto death: tarry ye here, and watch with me.*

He went a little farther into the Garden of Gethsemane, fell on His face, and began praying to Abba. He said:

*O my Father, if it be possible, let this cup pass from me: nevertheless not as I will, but as Thou wilt.*

He returned from praying in agony to find all three followers asleep. That's when He said to Peter:

***What, could ye not watch with me one hour?***

In this grief-stricken moment, Jesus asked His disciples to watch with Him while He travailed in prayer. But each time He returned, they were asleep.

This happens to the best of us. It is a prime example of the fact that even with the best intentions, we get tired, weary, hungry and sleepy. We often say that the only cure for sleep is sleep.

**Matthew 20: 5** *Again he went out about the sixth and ninth hour, and did likewise.*

These labourers being recruited at the various hours in the parable were just as human as the disciples. Imagine this! By 3 p.m., those who started working at 6 a.m. and 9 a.m., had accomplished nine and six hours of labour, respectively. Those who came in at noon had already worked three hours. They, too, were getting tired, but guess what? The workday was not over, and the harvest was far from being reaped.

So, again, the Master of the vineyard went back to the drawing board. He checked the number of hours remaining in the day and again compared it with the portion of the field that remained unharvested.

From His assessment of the situation, He saw the necessity to recruit more labourers. And He did, repeating the employment procedures used with the previous sets of workers. These also agreed to the terms and conditions, and with those crucial matters settled, they went to work at the ninth hour or 3 p.m.

Apparently, these are now the freshest and most energetic set of workers. They are seemingly carrying the greatest part of the workload at this juncture.

Watch this! There are now four different sets of labourers in the vineyard and four different sets of contractual agreements for each set of workers.

Remember now, one set of labourers would have already worked from 6 a.m. to 3p.m. One set from 9 a.m. to 3p.m. Another from noon to 3 p.m. and a fourth set would just be joining the workforce. All the labourers would continue working from 3 to 6 p.m.

Naturally, these labourers would have begun to socialize and share information about their employment arrangements and expectations at the end of the workday. This is common practice among employees.

Workers start out being strangers, but after a period of association, they begin to discover what they have in common. Eventually, cliques are formed within the workforce. As we say in Jamaica, 'Birds of a feather flock together'. How do you think demonstrations or strikes begin?

In wisdom, the master of the vineyard had done his due diligence and ensured that there was an agreement between himself and each worker before they started working. Today, the same principles have been inked into legal documents called contracts.

There are also government ministries which provide guidelines for procurement of workers. It details what should be in a contract and in the event, the rights of either the employer or employee are violated, legal actions can be taken.

Three hours now remained in the workday. Although the last set to be recruited might have been full of energy, it wouldn't be surprising for thoughts or discussions to arise among the labourers about expected remunerations at the close of the workday.

As in the physical, so it is in the spiritual. We enter the Kingdom of God at various hours of the harvest. God promises to reward every man according to their work. Let us, therefore, work while it is day, regardless of the time we entered the vineyard.

So far, we have discovered that each hour that the master recruited labourers for his physical vineyard in the parable, a similar recruitment took place in the kingdom of God. The ninth hour was no exception.

## THE NINTH HOUR OUTPOURING

### Acts 3: 1-9

*1 Now Peter and John went up together into the temple at the hour of prayer, being the ninth hour.*

*2 And a certain man lame from his mother's womb was carried, whom they laid daily at the gate of the temple which is called Beautiful, to ask alms of them that entered into the temple;*

*3 Who seeing Peter and John about to go into the temple asked an alms.*

*4 And Peter, fastening his eyes upon him with John, said, Look on us.*

*5 And he gave heed unto them, expecting to receive something of them.*

*6 Then Peter said, Silver and gold have I none; but such as I have give I thee: In the name of Jesus Christ of Nazareth rise up and walk.*

*7 And he took him by the right hand, and lifted him up: and immediately his feet and ankle bones received strength.*

*8 And he leaping up stood, and walked, and entered with them into the temple, walking, and leaping, and praising God.*

*9 And all the people saw him walking and praising God.*

The hour of prayer was the ninth hour of the day or 3 p.m. At this moment, yet another manifestation of the power of God and revelation of Jesus Christ occurred.

The second set that entered the Kingdom of God experienced the baptism of the Holy Ghost. The third set experienced true worship. This fourth set, at the hour of prayer, experienced the manifestation of the gift of healing.

After the healing power of Jesus was revealed, as with the prior manifestations, a revival followed. This mighty move of God resulted in another great harvest of souls. The number was approximately five thousand.

Peter and John preached to the crowd, which was filled with wonder and amazement. Their minds were blown by the manifestation of the healing power of God. The message of the Kingdom of God and Jesus Christ was preached to them, and they were converted.

This revelation landed Peter and John in jail. But the joy of the harvest of five thousand souls reduced the unpleasant experiences of incarceration to nothing. This was definitely not the last time that God's power was revealed and souls were added to the Kingdom of God.

So too, the persecution of God's vessels continues. Look out! When God's power begins to manifest through you, the religious folks come after you. They will stop at nothing to silence you. They don't worry about your preaching, but once the power of God is demonstrated and the sick are being healed, watch it!

You should, however, not be deterred by the persecution. Instead, remember Jesus' promise in Matthew 5:11 and follow His instruction in verse 12:

*11 Blessed are ye, when men shall revile you, and persecute you, and say all manner of evil against you falsely, for my sake.*

*12 Rejoice, and be exceeding glad: for great is your reward in heaven: for so persecuted they the prophets which were before you.*

# Chapter 6

# The Eleventh Hour of The Day

**Matthew 20:6-16**

*6 And about the eleventh hour he went out, and found others standing idle, and saith unto them, Why stand ye here all the day idle?*

*7 They say unto him, Because no man hath hired us. He saith unto them, Go ye also into the vineyard; and whatsoever is right, that shall ye receive.*

*8 So when even was come, the lord of the vineyard saith unto his steward, Call the labourers, and give them their hire, beginning from the last unto the first.*

*9 And when they came that were hired about the eleventh hour, they received every man a penny.*

*10 But when the first came, they supposed that they should have received more; and they likewise received every man a penny.*

*11 And when they had received it, they murmured against the goodman of the house,*

*12 Saying, These last have wrought but one hour, and thou hast made them equal unto us, which have borne the burden and heat of the day.*

*13 But he answered one of them, and said, Friend, I do thee no wrong: didst not thou agree with me for a penny?*

*14 Take that thine is and go thy way: I will give unto this last, even as unto thee.*

*15 Is it not lawful for me to do what I will with mine own? Is thine eye evil, because I am good?*

*16 So the last shall be first, and the first last: for many be called, but few chosen.*

The goodman of the vineyard recruited labourers for the fifth time within the workday. He was determined to reap the harvest at all costs. This time, He employed reapers at the eleventh and final hour of the workday. It's no coincidence that the fifth set of workers were entering the vineyard at 5 o'clock.

Notice that the previous intake of labourers was recruited at three-hour intervals. Now it had just been two hours since the last recruitment was made, at three o'clock. But the master was back in the streets, looking for reapers.

This final set of labourers were persons he found idling by the wayside. He enquired of them their reason for idling, and they said no one offered them work. So, He invited them to come and work for Him.

These are the eleventh-hour labourers. The eleventh hour is five o'clock in the afternoon or 5:00 p.m. I call this fifth set of labourers the five o'clock crew. This is the set that was surrounded by controversy at the end of the day.

These were seemingly idlers who were by the wayside for eleven hours of the workday. During this time, four sets of workers had arrived in the vineyard between 6 a.m. and 3 p.m. Now, based on the time this set came into the vineyard, they would only be working for one hour.

5:00 p.m. means that there is only one hour before dark, one hour before the workday is over. The five o'clock crew was different from all the other workers. They were previously overlooked by employers. And now that they are employed, they have but a short time to get the job done.

They seized the opportunity and began to work assiduously. Their motivation, work ethics and attitude must have caught the attention of the master. He rewarded them as much as he paid those who worked longer hours.

Apparently, the workers were paid in view of each other, from the last workers to the first. Everyone received the same salary, regardless of the number of hours they spent in the vineyard.

This angered the first set of workers, who assumed that they would have got higher wages than the five o'clock crew, since they entered the workforce at daybreak. The Bible says that they murmured against the master, who in turn reminded them of the mutual agreement they had.

He dismissed their claims with a sharp rebuke and made it clear that His actions were legal. They were also reminded that He was at liberty to spend his money as it pleased Him. He highlighted their covetousness and taught them an unorthodox principle.

This principle is at the centre of great grace and can be found in **Matthew 20:16.** *So the last shall be first, and the first last: for many be called, but few chosen.*

The lessons learnt from this parable are many and varied. In the natural, we are reminded that we ought to be focused on fulfilling our commitments and to avoid covetousness.

Spiritually speaking, we are all labourers in God's vineyard. Whatever we do, we do unto the Lord. He is the ultimate rewarder, and He pays us according to our works, whether it be good or evil, whether noticeable or unnoticeable to man.

God knows our hearts and judges our motives. He is very passionate about reaping the end-time harvest of souls and is looking for labourers who share His passion. Let us labour with this knowledge that we are in the final moments of the last hour of the day. Night is about to come when no man can work.

Where are the members of the five o'clock crew?

## THE FINAL HOUR OUTPOURING

There is a five o'clock crew! An eleventh-hour generation! And there is an eleventh-hour outpouring! This is the word for Two Thousand and Twenty-Five.

You might be wondering, what happens at 5 p.m. This is the hour that God is setting believers on fire to reap the end time harvest. He is setting the church ablaze to push back every attack; and empowering them with Dunamis to deal with every warfare.

This is the hour of great grace. It's the hour when we are being equipped to deal with every demonic power.

Here, all the outpourings are combined and released in the church.

Supernatural fire! Exusia fire is available to the people of God in this hour! In this season, walk in the fire! In this eleventh hour, walk with the fire!

The spirit of Gideon is rising in this hour to deal with the Amalekites. They shall be defeated before God's people again. We are taking back everything that the Midianites took from us.

Look out, church world! The five o'clock crew is coming! Look out! Watch out, religious world! The eleventh-hour group is coming!

Are you in it? This is the year that grace is going to hit many who are idling by the wayside and bring them into the Kingdom of God. Look out! God says that you have not seen anything yet.

I am very excited about what God is doing in this hour. Moreso, I am humbled and privileged to witness and participate in the end-time revival. God continues to manifest His power and reveal Himself to us.

I am labouring earnestly while anticipating His soon return. If you are too, shout 'Hallelujah!' Shout 'Thank You Jesus!' You ought to be excited that God has reserved you for this hour. You could not have been born in any other hour of the church age. Get excited about what God is going to use you to do in this hour.

Glory! Thank You Jesus! He is worthy of all the honour and the praise. As an unorthodox preacher, I don't mind taking a praise break while writing. I do the same when I am preaching, teaching, driving or even conducting business.

I don't know about you, but the Dunamis inside me has a way of exploding at unexpected times and I just got to let it out. I know that Jeremiah could relate. David, Paul, and Silas could, too. I am experiencing one of those explosions right now, as God reveals some of what He is doing in this hour. How about you?

Hallelujah! Hallelujah! Hallelujah!
Glory to the Most High God!
His name is Jesus!

God is moving by His Spirit in a mighty way in this hour!

I feel Him moving all over me!
I can't explain it,
But I've got to express it!
Hallelujah!
If you feel it, don't quench it!
Praise Him anytime, anywhere.
He is worthy of all our praise.
Hallelujah!
Come on Shabach the King of kings!
Yadah the Lord of lords!

I am glad that you have reached the eleventh-hour outpouring.

You are at the right place at the right time for your miracle!

You are at the right place at the right time for your breakthrough!

Go ahead and clap your hands!
Open your mouth!
Shout a high praise!
C'mon, give God one more shout of praise!
Shout Hallelujah!
Shout Glory Hallelujah!
Shout Thank You Jesus!
There is a five o'clock crew!
There is an eleventh-hour people!
There is a final hour outpouring!
Praise God for victory in Jesus' name.

The remainder of this book is for those who are anticipating the Lord's move in this hour. This is for those who are awaiting the day when He bursts open the eastern sky to rapture His children.

To you, I say, welcome to this hour! I want you to know that God still speaks! Contrary to what many believe, God is still on the move. He is still working miracles, and the Kingdom of God is forcefully advancing, despite the violence.

At the end of Two Thousand and Twenty-Four, I recalled a few of the things God showed me that came to pass. Among them was the release of a popular entertainer after he confessed that God is real.

At the time this book was written, He was not yet saved. Some might be condemnatory of his current lifestyle, because they are ignorant of God's timing and process. But I praise God for this mighty move and pray for his salvation. The entertainer confessed that he met

God while being incarcerated and that the encounter changed his life forever.

This is a prime example of some of the types of persons God is saving in the eleventh hour. Matthew 3:9-10 addresses God's response to unfruitfulness. He said that He would do whatever it takes to raise up children to Abraham. If it requires using stones, He would do it.

'Stones' here, refers to persons who are known to be hard hearted. Persons whose lifestyles, like Paul, were anti-church, persecuting the people of God and rebelling against God's laws. I am believing God, that as they enter the Kingdom of God, they are going to bring thousands of lost souls to Jesus.

God does not desire the death of sinners, but that all should come to repentance and live. This should be the desire and prayer of every Christian. It's time to reach those on the byways and hedges and bring them into the vineyard.

Anything is possible at the eleventh and final hour. God remains a God of the impossible. The final hour is the hour for the final revival before the rapturing of the church.

Salvation of the chiefest of sinners who truly believes, is still possible. Healing and deliverance are still available. In this season, the end time harvest of the Gentiles is being reaped. God is fast forwarding His mandate and doing a quick work.

If you are going to see the miracle that you have been praying and believing for, now is the time to lift your faith to see its manifestation.

The wealth of the wicked is being transferred to the righteous in this hour. It's the hour to reap the spoils, both in the natural and spiritual. God did promise us a harvest in this life and in the life to come, eternal life.

Whatever is to be reaped in the natural, the time is now. Many believers, like the disciples, are overly concerned about the returns on their sacrifice of earthly goods to follow Christ.

In **Mark 10:29-31**

*29 And Jesus answered and said, Verily I say unto you, There is no man that hath left house, or brethren, or sisters, or father, or mother, or wife, or children, or lands, for my sake, and the gospel's,*

*30 But he shall receive an hundredfold now in this time, houses, and brethren, and sisters, and mothers, and children, and lands, with persecutions; and in the world to come eternal life.*

*31 But many that are first shall be last; and the last first.*

Now is the time! But don't forget the persecutions! Notice that the persecutions that the eleventh-hour workers received, came from the first set of workers in the vineyard. So, don't be surprised that you will be ridiculed by religious folks, including your church brethren.

There are many who want to dictate to the Master, how to bless His people and who deserves to be blessed. Many wish that God would give them the power to determine who is saved and who is damned.

The eleventh hour is an action-packed hour in both realms. The enemy knows that his time is coming to an end and so spiritual wickedness is at an all-time high. This is the hour when we are going to see and hear of catastrophes like never before. There are going to be more wars and rumours of wars. More "plan-demics" will be released.

Be not alarmed children of God! For God has not forgot His people. While the enemy is increasingly violent against the kingdom of God, the church is beginning to experience an extraordinary supernatural outpouring to counteract all the onslaughts of the enemy.

This hour requires the wisdom and vigilance of the warriors God chose to accompany Gideon to defeat the enemy. They were quenching their thirst by lapping like a dog. In this way they would be refreshed while remaining on the lookout for the enemy.

We too have so much to do in this final hour. While we are refreshing our souls from the eleventh-hour outpouring of the Holy Spirit, we also need to be reaping those souls in the end time revival.

While we are reaping the hundred-fold harvest God promised us in this life, we must brace ourselves for the persecutions. And above all, in this hour of great grace, we must be mindful of the danger of continuing in sin, because of the abundance of God's grace. Therefore, let us mortify the deeds of the body; sanctify ourselves that we will reap eternal life.

Let us pause to pray for all those of us living in this eleventh and final hour of the day

# PRAYER

*Eternal God, our Father, our King, our Master, our Redeemer, our Keeper and our Saviour;*
*God who declared, 'Let there be light' and there was light.*
*God of Abraham, Isaac and of Jacob;*
*We give You praise and honour.*
*Lord, we lift You up.*
*We exalt and magnify You.*
*As You have brought us to this hour, we thank You.*
*Father, You are gathering Your people together for this eleventh-hour outpouring according to Your word:*
*The scepter shall not depart from Judah, nor a lawgiver from between his feet, until Shiloh comes, and unto Him shall the gathering of the people be.*
*Lord, no man can come to You except Your Spirit draws them.*
*Thank You Holy Spirit for bringing us together.*
*Many would like to be a part of this move Lord,*
*But they are somewhere in bondage.*
*Some are experiencing depression, sadness and oppression, but they desire to praise You.*
*But they can't do so Lord because there is a spirit that is blocking them.*
*It is not in man to order his own steps.*
*And so, Lord we pray for their deliverance.*
*While we praise You for Your great grace and many mercies towards us.*

*We ask You, please Holy Spirit to speak to those who are eager to hear a word from You.*
*Speak to Your church.*
*Speak to Your people.*
*Continue to sit upon me Holy Ghost.*
*Trust me with Your anointing one more time, Holy Spirit.*
*Please, sit upon me.*
*Let Your efficacious blood cover everyone praying this prayer.*
*Let the blood of Jesus Christ of Nazareth be poured upon us.*
*From the crown of our head unto the soles of our feet.*
*Lord, use me to write upon the hearts of Your people.*
*Arise in this final hour Holy Spirit!*
*Let all Your enemies be scattered!*
*Give victory to Your people.*
*While they read, I pray that you will save, heal and deliver.*
*Set somebody free, Holy Spirit.*
*Oh Lord, we look to You because You are our only source.*
*Have Your way Jesus!*
*Let high-ranking angels have free course in this hour.*
*Let them do warfare on behalf of the Church.*
*Let them give victory to Your people, in the name of Jesus Christ. AMEN*

Father, we thank You, because victory is in Your precious blood. Victory is in the name of Jesus Christ.
Come on now!

Throw your head back!
Open your mouth and praise Your Maker!
Hallelujah!
Thank You Jesus!

# Chapter 7

# The First Watch of The Night

In previous chapters, the focus was on activities during the day. These are the hours when we are awake and busy with our daily activities. This usually requires physical strength and mental alertness, leaving one exhausted at the end of the day.

As the physical man goes to rest, the spirit man becomes active and our dependence on God to watch over us increases to an all-time high. During the night, we are surrounded by darkness and evil is at its peak.

But thanks be to God! We serve a God who does not put on pyjamas! He neither slumbers nor sleeps. Hallelujah! He is the God who works the night shift. We don't have to worry! We don't have to fret! The darkness is as the light to Him, so we only need to place our spirit in His capable hands and let nature take its course. Rest!

However, to sustain victory in the waking hours, we are sometimes awakened from our sleep to pray. This is a call we should never ignore. Our response to this call could determine whether we experience victory or defeat at daybreak.

### Lamentations 2:19
*Arise, cry out in the night: in the beginning of the watches pour out thine heart like water before the face of the Lord: lift up thy hands toward Him for the life of thy young children, that faint for hunger in the top of every street.*

In biblical and ancient Jewish culture, the night, like the day, was divided into four distinct watches of three hours each. The first century Romans also had a similar practice.

The curious person that I am, I began to research the various watches to unearth:

1. why they were so divided;
2. what happens at each watch and;
3. the spiritual significance of each watch.

This research heightened my awareness that even in prayer, timing is everything. I received a clearer understanding of the need to pray without ceasing. For a victorious walk with God, each believer should have a set hour of prayer both night and day. All these are important to remain relevant and vigilant in this hour.

Not only that, when you pray at the different watches, it is of vital importance that you understand how to pray and what kind of prayers to pray. Put another way, certain prayers should be prayed at certain times for effectiveness. It is one thing for a righteous man to pray; but it is another thing to pray effectual, fervent prayers. The Bible lets us know that the latter availeth much.

You don't want to have spent hours in prayer, only to discover that you were praying amiss. For example, when you are under certain attacks and dealing with a particular type of warfare, you need to be aware of the best time to pray.

If you are up against principalities and powers, you should know that the day prayer does not really deal with those spirits. Come with me now! If you are dealing with those spirits, you need to know at what time of the night you need to get up and pray.

Each watch corresponds with a specific timeframe and has great spiritual significance. Understanding these watches enriches our prayer life, spiritual warfare strategies, and intimacy with God.

Jesus pointed out the four watches of the night as He admonished His disciples and by extension, everyone to always remain watchful.

**Mark 13:35-37**
*35 Watch ye therefore: for ye know not when the master of the house cometh, at even, or at midnight, or at the cockcrowing, or in the morning.*
*36 Lest coming suddenly he find you sleeping.*
*37 And what I say unto you I say unto all, Watch.*

The concept of watches was designed for the safety of Israel against their physical enemies. These included both people and beasts. However, it was also customary for the Jewish people to pray at these watches. This meant that in Israel, someone was watching and praying throughout every watch of the night.

In **Isaiah 62:6** the Lord says:
*I have set watchmen upon thy walls, O Jerusalem, which shall never hold their peace day nor night: ye that make mention of the Lord, keep not silence.*

So it was with Israel, so it is with Christian warriors. God has assigned prayer watches to believers. Fortunately, we aren't always shown the pending dangers because it can cripple us with fear. However, they can and will be aborted if we pray without ceasing and pray all types of prayers.

As we examine each watch more closely, I encourage you to schedule the reading on each watch for a period within the actual watch. Develop the habit of praying appropriate prayers at each watch according to your knowledge of the watch and your circumstances.

Most believers receive an unction from the Holy Spirit at least once in the night to get up and pray. Obedience to this prompting usually requires sacrifice. Most people will agree that sleep is sweet, especially after a hard day's work. However, don't ignore these promptings from the Holy Spirit. Once you recognise that you are constantly being awakened at a particular hour of the night, stop wondering why. Just pray!

The first watch of the night is from 6 to 9 p.m. and is called the evening watch. This is a moment characterized by a feeling of being overwhelmed after a day's work. Therefore, the focus of the evening watch is usually on reflection and spiritual foundation.

The first watch of the night marks the beginning of a new day in Jewish reckoning, starting at sunset. You will recall that **Genesis 1:5** informs us that, *"… the evening and the morning were the first day."* So, this watch is a time for reflection on God's faithfulness throughout the day and laying a spiritual foundation for the night. In **Psalm 141:2**, David prays, *"May my prayer be set before You like incense, the lifting up of my hands like the evening sacrifice."*

Reflections of this nature lead to a time of thanksgiving for divine providence and protection. **Psalm 92:1-2** says:

*1 It is a good thing to give thanks unto the Lord, and to sing praises unto Thy name, O Most High:*
*2 To shew forth Thy lovingkindness in the morning and Thy faithfulness every night.*

As we prepare to rest from the day's labour, believers should schedule time for personal and family devotion. During this time, we should give thanks, make confessions and seek healing and restoration.

At this watch, we should also reflect on God's word and pray for the night ahead. All fear should be renounced as we seek divine protection. Prayers should be made to establish spiritual covering over our family and endeavours. We should also pray for peace and victory over the works of darkness.

Psalm 91 is a powerful prayer for believers to pray at this watch. It speaks of God's divine protection in all watches and gives comfort to the believer as the physical man loses consciousness to sleep.

### Psalm 91

*1 He that dwelleth in the secret place of the most High shall abide under the shadow of the Almighty.*

*2 I will say of the Lord, He is my refuge and my fortress: my God; in Him will I trust.*

*3 Surely He shall deliver thee from the snare of the fowler, and from the noisome pestilence.*

*4 He shall cover thee with His feathers, and under His wings shalt thou trust: His truth shall be thy shield and buckler.*

*5 Thou shalt not be afraid for the terror by night; nor for the arrow that flieth by day;*

*6 Nor for the pestilence that walketh in darkness; nor for the destruction that wasteth at noonday.*

*7 A thousand shall fall at thy side, and ten thousand at thy right hand; but it shall not come nigh thee.*

*8 Only with thine eyes shalt thou behold and see the reward of the wicked.*

*9 Because thou hast made the Lord, which is my refuge, even the most High, thy habitation;*

*10 There shall no evil befall thee, neither shall any plague come nigh thy dwelling.*

*11 For He shall give His angels charge over thee, to keep thee in all thy ways.*

*12 They shall bear thee up in their hands, lest thou dash thy foot against a stone.*

*13 Thou shalt tread upon the lion and adder: the young lion and the dragon shalt thou trample under feet.*

*14 Because he hath set his love upon Me, therefore will I deliver him: I will set him on high, because he hath known My name.*

*15 He shall call upon Me, and I will answer him: I will be with him in trouble; I will deliver him, and honour him.*

*16 With long life will I satisfy him, and shew him My salvation.*

# Chapter 8

# The Second Watch of The Night

The second watch of the night begins at 9 p.m. and finishes at midnight. It is called the midnight watch. In the Old Testament, God gave Israel victory through Gideon during this watch. It was at midnight that he and his men engaged their enemies in warfare.

**Judges 7:19-21**
*19 So Gideon, and the hundred men that were with him, came unto the outside of the camp in the beginning of the middle watch, and they had but newly set the watch: and they blew the trumpets, and brake the pitchers that were in their hands.*

*20 And the three companies blew the trumpets and brake the pitchers, and held the lamps in their left hands, and the trumpets in their right hands to blow withal: and they cried, The sword of the Lord, and of Gideon.*

*21 And they stood every man in his place round about the camp: and all the host ran, and cried, and fled.*

I told you that even in the night watches, timing is everything. Because they blew the trumpet at the right time, the enemies fled. At this watch the Lord set every man's sword against his fellow. God let the enemies turn against themselves and destroyed themselves.

By now, you should begin to grasp the importance of praying at the midnight watch and what prayers to pray in order to be victorious over your enemies. You must be conscious of the kind of attack that you are facing too.

The Midianites, Amalekites, and children of the east were as grasshoppers in multitude. This means that the Israelites were outnumbered, having only thirty-two thousand men. I was very careful not to refer to them as warriors because as God began to scan them, we realized that most of them were fearful.

Understandably, being fearful was a natural initial response in this situation. However, despite their fears from being outnumbered, God said to Gideon, the people that you have with you are too many. Send home all who are fearful and afraid.

Do you know how many went home? Twenty-two thousand went home, leaving only ten thousand men. As ridiculous as it sounds, God told Gideon that there were still too many men, so he was to test the rest by the brook. Gideon was to keep only those who lapped like a dog.

This reduced the warriors to three hundred men. That's a little less than ten percent of the original number. Finally, God was satisfied that He had an army of real warriors! To this small army God gave the instructions for warfare through Gideon.

The rules of engagement for this battle were simple. Each warrior was to have a trumpet in one hand and a light in the other. Any idea why? Let me tell you - you can't blow the trumpet and be in darkness. You need light while you blow thc trumpet.

In the New Testament - **Matthew 25:1-6**, Jesus said:

*1 Then shall the kingdom of heaven be likened unto ten virgins, which took their lamps, and went forth to meet the bridegroom.*

*2 And five of them were wise, and five were foolish.*

*3 They that were foolish took their lamps, and took no oil with them:*

*4 But the wise took oil in their vessels with their lamps.*

*5 While the bridegroom tarried, they all slumbered and slept.*

*6 And at midnight there was a cry made, Behold, the bridegroom cometh; go ye out to meet him.*

Watch this! in both scenarios, at midnight, there was a shout; a cry. In the first scripture, at the blowing of the trumpet there was a war cry.

In the latter scripture, at the blowing of the trumpet there was a cry to arise and go to meet the Master. At midnight, the bridegroom was on His way to meet His bride.

According to scriptures, the midnight watch was the time Jesus prayed in the Garden of Gethsemane. This watch is characterized by weakness in the flesh from being tired, contrasted by a willingness of the spirit, which is active at midnight.

At this juncture there is a war between the flesh and the spirit to pray. **Ephesians 6:12** reminds us:

*For we wrestle not against flesh and blood, but against principalities, against powers, against the rulers of the darkness of this world, against spiritual wickedness in high places.*

The second watch is a time of heightened spiritual activity. This watch often represents a time of battle against demonic forces. Just as it was with Jesus, the enemy wants us to surrender our spirits to him so that he can use it to accomplish his evil plans in the earth.

Jesus was battling whether to fulfil His mandate by going to the cross or to forfeit His assignment. His decision would determine if His flesh would remain alive or if it would die so that the glorified body would be revealed. The latter was necessary to bring us hope through redemption.

It was a very difficult decision, and so, the Son of man prayed,

*O my Father, if it be possible, let this cup pass from me: nevertheless not as I will, but as Thou wilt.* **Matthew 26:39.**

We all face life-altering decisions in the midnight of our lives too. That's when the Holy Spirit unctions us to pray but the flesh wants to sleep. This battle continues to rage until we either give in to sleep or get up and pray. Whichever wins, possibly determines what happens in the remaining watches of the night and later in the day.

As the forces of evil begin to launch their midnight attacks, their main objective is to hold our bodies captive in sleep. This hinders our spirits from engaging in intercessory prayer. A spirit unyielded to God in prayer at midnight can be a powerful weapon in the hand of the devil to carry out attacks on others, including believers.

This is not a watch to be ignored! It is a watch to resist evil influences. A time for intercession, deliverance, and breakthrough prayers. Paul and Silas were cognizant of the power of midnight prayer and praise. I wonder if they were meditating on this scripture while they were in prison. **Psalm 119:62** says, *At midnight I rise to give You thanks for Your righteous laws.*

**Acts 16:25-26** let us know their response to the Holy Spirit's midnight unction and God's response to their actions:

*25 And at midnight Paul and Silas prayed, and sang praises unto God: and the prisoners heard them.*

*26 And suddenly there was a great earthquake so that the foundations of the prison were shaken: and immediately all the doors were opened, and everyone's bands were loosed.*

In **Exodus 12:29** also, we see how God killed all the firstborn of Egypt at midnight. This is yet another demonstration of His power over oppression. Numerous victories have been recorded in scriptures which God gave to His people at midnight. This should be enough to encourage us to engage in praise and warfare prayers during the midnight hours.

Thanks be to God! By God's grace, King Jesus Pentecostal Fellowship continues to be fully engaged and active during this watch. It is one of the actions of the ministry which garners the most attention and criticism. Unbelievably, but not surprisingly, religious folks are the main complainants and critics. They are furious and offended that we are always praising and worshipping at the midnight watch.

In their opinion, we lack wisdom, but it is quite the contrary. However, we are undaunted! We are not perturbed because we know what prayer does at this hour. We pray for those who are oppressed and in bondage. We declare and decree God's promises as we intercede for nations, leaders, and families in turmoil.

Yes! Unashamedly, we pray and praise God for victory over all evils at work in the midnight hours. And we continually witness God's mighty power being demonstrated, as He pushes back catastrophes and cancels assignments from hell. All in response to blowing the trumpet and releasing a war cry in the midnight watch.

Glory be to God for all the midnight watchers and warriors! I cover you from every attack right now! Do not get weary in well doing for in due season, God says, you shall reap your reward, if you do not faint. Those who have been ignoring the call, get up! It's high time to awake from your slumber and burn the midnight oil in Jesus' name!

Get up! Blow the trumpet and sound the alarm!

# Chapter 9

# The Third Watch of The Night

The third watch is from twelve midnight to 3 a.m. It is called Cock Crowing Watch. This is said to be the darkest part of the night. This is a time for spiritual warfare, but also of divine judgment. It is often associated with spiritual battles and divine intervention.

During the third watch of the night, witchcraft is at its peak, as the enemies conduct operations to alter people's destinies. Evil-doers believe that they are untouchable during these times. At daybreak they gloat about the wickedness done in the dark and exalt themselves by holding others down.

But I heard Daniel say that Nebuchadnezzar was upon his palace wall and he was speaking proudly. He said, "Look at this beautiful Babylon that I have built." We learn also that the moment he uttered those words, the watchers heard him and reported to the Lord of Hosts.

The watchers are angels who are on assignment at certain watches. While you are sleeping, they are watching. Yes! While you are asleep in your bed, they are watching over you.

They are mentioning your name to your father. David says in

**Psalm 34:7** *The angel of the Lord encampeth round about them that fear Him, and delivereth them.*

They are at work throughout these watches as we have read in **Psalm 91**. In verse one, the Psalmist declares:

*He that dwelleth in the secret place of the Most High shall abide under the shadow of the Almighty.*

The watchers are on assignment to ensure that you and I are protected from the wicked.

*For He shall give His angels charge over thee, to keep thee in all thy ways. They shall bear thee up in their hands, lest thou dash thy foot against a stone.*

When our enemies speak, the watchers listen and record what they are saying. While we sleep, someone is in the graveyard with our names and items of clothing. Someone is heading to a remote community to engage the services of an "obeah man" or woman to cast witchcraft spells on you or your loved ones. Somebody is trying to sabotage your business, trying to get you out of that job, or blocking your breakthrough or promotion.

This is an evil world and we dare not underestimate the abilities of principalities and powers. The rulers of darkness of this world are in full operation during this watch. This is the key moment when spiritual wickedness goes on in high places.

Evil altars are erected at the third watch and plans are set in motion against believers as they sleep. Witches and warlocks are summoned during these dark hours. But the watchers are also on assignment. As they nudge us, we need to get up and launch a counterattack against the forces of darkness.

If we refuse to engage in spiritual warfare during this watch, our lives and that of our families, friends, destiny helpers and loved ones can become a nightmare. Although the physical body is asleep, the spirit man is alert. Guided by the Holy Spirit, we are equipped for battle and are guaranteed victory over our enemies, in Jesus' name.

Nebuchadnezzar encountered the watchers and his pride led to judgment from them. He got a dream which troubled his spirit. He had seen a watcher come down from heaven and gave instructions for a great tree to be hewn down.

He had called for the magicians, soothsayers, Chaldeans, and astrologers to interpret his dream. They could not interpret it, and he decided to kill them all.

He sent for Daniel to interpret his dream. Daniel explained to him that there is a God who lives in heaven and runs earth. He raises up kingdoms and He pull down kingdoms. He raises up kings, and He pulls down kings.

Daniel told him that the dream meant that the watchers are watching him and that if his pride goes unchecked, it was going to bring him down. Daniel advised him to stop the bragging as he was exalting himself above God. He warned Nebuchadnezzar to stop acting as if he runs things.

The wise man Solomon warns in **Proverbs 16:18**.

*Pride goeth before destruction and an haughty spirit before a fall.*

Like Nebuchadnezzar, the enemies of God and His people, often consider themselves untouchable because of their associations with evil powers. They deny that there is only one God and even purport that they themselves are gods.

However, their claims do not negate the fact that there is only one God. He is the God of heaven and He alone runs things. In this lies the confidence of every believer, that our God is omnipresent, omniscient, and omnipotent. Therefore, we just need to obey Him and pray. He will protect and defend His children.

When Nebuchadnezzar got the memo, for a brief moment he humbled himself. Like many of us, he became complacent after a while and took the grace and mercy of God towards him for granted. It amazes me sometimes how defiant evil workers can be. So many times, the writings are on the wall that God is about to rain His judgment on them because of their constant attacks on His children. They relent for a while but soon return, at times even more ruthless than before. They mistake the watchers' silence for their absence. But don't be fooled, God is a God of time and chance.

It is important to remind yourself of this fact now and again. Let somebody else know too, that you don't run things. A God run things!

Nebuchadnezzar was in Babylon and God's people were from all the way in Jerusalem. Even though the house of God was in Jerusalem, He still runs things everywhere. So, while this big, bad king Nebuchadnezzar was talking proudly, the angels of the Lord were right there in Babylon, watching his every move and recording every word. Even the idle words are being recorded by the watchers, and they must be accounted for.

After Daniel warned him, he said alright, I am going to behave myself - and he actually did for a while. But his memory was short. The Bible says that a year later, Nebuchadnezzar got up, walked onto his balcony and viewed one of what is now the renowned seven wonders of the world.

Then he began to speak proudly again. According to **Daniel 4:30**, he boasted:

*Is not this great Babylon, that I have built for the house of the kingdom by the might of my power, and for the honour of my majesty?*

The word of God says that,

*while the word was in the king's mouth, there fell a voice from heaven, saying, O king Nebuchadnezzar, to thee it is spoken; The kingdom is departed from thee.*

*And they shall drive thee from men, and thy dwelling shall be with the beasts of the field: they shall make thee to eat grass as oxen, and seven times shall pass over thee, until thou know that the most High ruleth in the kingdom of men, and giveth it to whomsoever he will.*

Unfortunately, God was not so merciful this time. The watchers hew down the great king Nebuchadnezzar immediately. He lost his sanity and for seven years, he was exiled from humanity.

He was driven from men, and did eat grass as oxen, and his body was wet with the dew of heaven, till his hairs were grown like eagles' feathers, and his nails like birds' claws, according to the word of the Lord.

He was a madman until he acknowledged that there is one God, who sits high and looks low - until he realized that God controls every man's key, until he admitted that when God shuts a door, can no man open it and when He opens a door, no man can shut it.

In the past, witchcraft was not only illegal but something to be ashamed of. Not so in the twenty-first century. Our leaders are now advocating for witchcraft to be legalized. They can often be seen and heard on social media platforms, proudly displaying and declaring their associations with evil powers.

Guard rings, necklaces, bracelets, and other objects given for good luck and protection from demonic forces, are now paraded on public display. During heightened political campaigns, political candidates can be seen attending rituals. Many say, "I went to seek help. I didn't do anything to anyone."

But I am here to warn everyone indulging in these works of darkness, THE WATCHERS ARE WATCHING YOU!

They were watching Saul, when he consulted the medium - the witch of Endor. They were watching king Nebuchadnezzar and believe it or not, they are watching you.

Repent! Judgment is at your door! Be wise! Take heed! That was a warning.

Believers do not fear those who use the third watch of the night to plot and plan evils against you. I have great news for you! The watchers are watching!

Throw your head back, open your mouth, and praise the most High God. Shout Hallelujah! Shout glory! Shout glory! Hallelujah! Shout thank you Jesus!

You realize by now that God wakes you up during this watch to do warfare. The watchers are working but you also need to do your part. Apostles, prophets, intercessors, gap standers, and burden bearers, this is your watch. It is the hour to pray. Get up and launch counter-attacks, opposing the plans of the enemies.

This is a dreadful watch! Terrorize the kingdom of darkness and release God's people. This is a strategic hour! God will wake you in these hours when the enemies are attacking your families, finances, health, destiny, and wealth.

Don't roll over and play dead! Do not cower in fear! Get up! Get on your knees and declare war! Wherever possible, join forces with another warrior. As you engage in spiritual warfare prayers, declare God's judgment on evil. Pray for revival and spiritual awakenings within the church as well as your community. Above all, ask God for wisdom and remain ready for His return.

The word of God says that one shall chase a thousand and two put ten thousand to flight. Get up and pray! Get up and pray! Get up and pray! Intercede until you get the victory! Remember that you are not fighting a losing battle. Victory is yours in Jesus' name.

# Chapter 10

# The Fourth Watch of The Night

Warring Your Enemies

The watchers on the night shift, control certain watches. They are not only warriors, some also come with your blessing. You can be in church for twenty years; thirty years and God is constantly visiting your home and you never met Him. God has visited believers several times during the night watches and they never discerned His presence.

The fourth watch is the final watch of the night. It begins at 3 a.m. and ends at 6 a.m. This happens to be daybreak or the dawning of a new day. It is a time for the manifestation of God's power and breakthrough.

During this watch, men sleep! And Jesus says in **Matthew 13:25**

*While men slept, his enemy came and sow tares among the wheat.* I

believe that Jesus was referring to this and the previous watch.

The fourth watch spells trouble. This is the watch when men are taken at unawares or off guard. During this watch, the most illegal and evil activities take place, especially criminal and violent acts. Both in the natural and spiritual, the activities of the fourth watch can determine what your day is going to be.

During this watch, the witches are climaxing their craft, and warlocks completing their assignments. At this watch, thieves break into houses and businesses.

According to Jewish theology, oral laws were passed down to Israel. It is believed that, even before that which was written when Moses came on the scene from Genesis to Deuteronomy, the Jews were transferring information from one generation to the other orally. This means that not everything that the Jews believed was written.

In their homes, they would constantly repeat vital information to their children. On the streets, they would repeat it among themselves. The Jews would have you know that when you go to sleep your natural ears go to sleep. Your ear gate is closed and therefore you are unable to hear in the physical realm. However, in the third and fourth watches, your spiritual ears are awakened.

One of the things the rabbis taught is that God visits earth at 3 a.m.

During this visit, it is believed that God releases a blessing and that this blessing flows over the earth between 3 a.m. and daybreak. This belief results in the Jews taking time out to pray during this watch seriously.

I believe that these angels are still visiting mankind today. If you are praying during this watch, these angels will release blessings in your home. I wonder if you are a believer that goes into prayer at 3 a.m.? Have you ever been led by God to get up and pray at 3 a.m.?

I asked these questions at one of our services and most hands were raised. Do you know why? That's because there is a nudging; a prompting from the Holy Ghost at this watch.

Long before I understood the significance of each watch and the importance of praying certain prayers at specific times, I would get up and pray at 3 a.m. nightly. One particular night I came in from church exhausted. I said, "Lord, I am so tired; please wake me at three o'clock."

I must have fallen into deep sleep almost immediately. At some point, I felt a poke in my side. I jumped out of my sleep and looked around to see who poked me. There was no one around. I knew for sure it was a finger that poked me. I sprang from the bed and looked at the clock. Guess what time it was? You guessed right, it was three o'clock on the dot!

I know that this experience is not unique to me. Many persons can relate to being awakened at a specific time of the night on a regular basis. If you didn't know why this happened, wonder no more. It is your hour of prayer.

I come to let you know that there is something about 3 a.m. to 6 a.m. But before I go further, please allow me to talk to you a little about prayer. What I have to say is very important; it's a revelation.

Jesus says in **Matthew 6:6:**

*When thou prayest, enter into thy closet, and when thou hast shut thy door, pray to thy Father which is in secret; and thy Father which seeth in secret shall reward thee openly.*

This means that Jesus rewards those who pray. In other words, God is saying that if you pray, there is a pay. He is going to bless you for praying.

There is a watch of the night; the most difficult time for anyone to pray. It's between 3 and 6 a.m. It is said that during this watch, "man" is asleep. I mean deep sleep.

However, I am calling someone who receives the anointing to pray at this watch to get up and pray. It was at this watch that Jesus was on the mountain praying. While in prayer, He perceived that the disciples were in trouble on the lake.

According to the scriptures, this situation was brought on by a contrary wind that was blowing in the midst of the lake. This teaches us that principalities and powers are at work during this hour.

Principalities and powers bring destruction during this watch. But thanks be to God, the man Christ Jesus was up praying. The Bible says, that He perceived that the disciples were in trouble.

From the mountain, down the hill. Then to the edge of the lake. From the edge of the lake to the middle of the lake. The troubled disciples looked to see who or what was in their space. It was Jesus! He had shown up in the midst of their trouble.

If you learn how to pray at this watch, you will receive revelations of persons who are going through hard times. You will get downloads in your spirit. That is why the devil does not want you to pray at this hour. He wants you to sleep throughout this watch.

Have you ever wondered why the enemies are so mad about the hours that King Jesus Pentecostal Fellowship members are worshipping, praying, and doing warfare? God has shown me on numerous occasions that during this watch, we are pushing back the forces of darkness.

I never quite understood why I prayed until daybreak most time. Now I realize that it is because of the calling on my life and the ministry that God has entrusted to me. He keeps me alert in the realms of the spirit during these hours. I have had "out of body" experiences during this watch. I have been taken to different homes, business places, and countries to do warfare.

Oftentimes as I come out of prayer at sunrise, I am exhausted. Many times, I sleep for the entire day to recover. That's how dangerous the fourth watch of the night is.

While men sleep, the enemy is busy. God has to have a man, a woman, a boy, or a girl who will watch. Are you that one? Are you called to be a watcher at the fourth watch of the night?

The devil doesn't want you to be in prayer during this watch because he knows pretty well that God downloads things in the supernatural to empower His people at this time.

If you ever learn to pray at this watch, your life will become easier. If you ever learn to pray at this watch, you will handle what the devil plans for tomorrow in the realms of the spirit in advance.

Jesus walked on water during this watch according to **Matthew 14:25-27:**

*25 And in the fourth watch of the night Jesus went unto them, walking on the sea.*

*26 And when the disciples saw Him walking on the sea, they were troubled, saying, It is a spirit; and they cried out for fear.*

*27 But straightway Jesus spake unto them, saying, Be of good cheer, it is I, be not afraid.*

Here He was demonstrating His power over nature and fear.

This watch is said to be the watch in which Jesus was resurrected from the dead, gaining victory over death, hell, and the grave. This represents God's power and the dawn of new beginnings.

**Psalm 30:5** says:
*For His anger endureth but a moment; in His favour is life: weeping may endure for a night, but joy cometh in the morning.*

This was one of Jesus' noted moments of prayer. **Mark 1:35:**

*And in the morning, rising up a great while before day, He went out, and departed into a solitary place, and there prayed.*

Likewise, during the fourth hour, we should pray for renewed strength, guidance, and clarity. We should declare the breaking of every chain and the light of God's truth. Additionally, we need to align with God's will for the new day.

### Exodus 14:24-25
*24 And it came to pass, that in the morning watch the Lord looked unto the host of the Egyptians through the pillar of fire and of cloud, and troubled the host of the Egyptians.*

*25 And took off their chariot wheels, that they drave them heavily: so that the Egyptians said, Let us flee from the face of Israel; for the Lord fighteth for them against the Egyptians.*

Let somebody know that the Lord is your battle axe. Yes! He fights for His children. God is a good God! At the fourth watch, God is moving on behalf of His church. We see from the scriptures that Egypt had the children of God under pressure. For years they had them in bondage.

But with a mighty hand and an outstretched arm, God delivered Israel. Now Israel is on the run. Moses had said to God, I am willing to go with these people out of Egypt, but I will not go alone. He said, "God, if you do not come with me, I will not go."

God told Moses that His angel will go with him as a pillar of fire by night and a pillar of cloud by day. He told Moses that he was to be careful because His name was in this angel.

So, God delivered Israel out of the hands of the Egyptians, and they set out for the Promised Land. But guess what? The Egyptians began to pursue the people of God.

God used the angel; in the night, he went before Israel as a pillar of fire to keep back the Egyptians. The fire gave Israel light and direction at night, while the enemies were in darkness. You cannot walk in a deserted place without electricity or some other form of light.

As Israel moved forward and day broke, the angel would shift from before them and go behind them as a pillar of cloud during the day to separate them from the view of the Egyptians. At all times Israel was able to keep moving, while the angel blocked their enemies.

While Egypt was beating the sun, Israel was getting shade. The pillar of cloud provided shade from the heat of the noonday sun. In that way they would not grow weary and faint in the desert.

While Egypt was in darkness, Israel was receiving light. While it is rough for the enemy, God is making a way for His Children. Can you testify that you have this blessed assurance that you are not alone because the angels of the Lord are with you.

David said: Surely goodness and mercy shall follow me all the days of my life. Hallelujah! Glory to God!

The Bible says that during the morning watch, between 3 and 6 a.m., the Lord looked upon the Egyptians through the pillar of fire and clouds.

What is the Bible saying, Apostle? The Bible lets us know that God, through the eyes of the angel looked at the Egyptians, which means the angel who was on watch was God's eyes in this situation. I know that this is too deep for some.

God saw that the Egyptians were gaining momentum and somehow, getting too close for comfort to the children of Israel. So too, my God has assigned angels to ensure that the enemy does not get too close to you. Don't worry!

God will never allow your enemies to overtake you. He will not allow your enemies to know everything. God is keeping them off.

God is backing them off. And should they ever come too close, He is going to intervene.

The word of God lets us know that when the angel realized that the Egyptians were too close to Israel, God began to trouble them. My God! Those obeah workers cannot pass their boundaries. There is a line of demarcation between you and them.

The haters at your workplace cannot pass their limit. There is an angel that is assigned to protect you; to direct you and ensure that the enemies keep their distance.

Watch this! the angel began to take off their chariot wheels. He began to slow down the enemies. Let somebody know that God says He is going to slow down your enemies. Can you find five people to give this rope of hope?

Go ahead and reassure them that they are not alone and God is going to slow down all the enemies that appear to be getting too close for their comfort. Sometimes, they are so close to you that they seem to be right at your heel. But, do not worry! I have a word from God for you.

God says that He is going to let their chariot wheels get heavy. Do you know what that meant for Israel? God paved the path for His children so that Israel was walking on solid ground.

When the angel discovered that the Egyptians were getting too close, he went underground and spilled some mud on the surface where the enemies' chariots were driving. So, while the children of God were moving comfortably on asphalt, the enemies were getting stuck in the mud.

This is not for those who do not want to hear what God is saying in this year of great grace. This is not for those who are not zealous to see the hand of God moving in the midst of the enemies in this season.

This is for the warriors! This is for the people of God! This is for those who need a word from God in the fourth watch; in the turbulent times when principalities and powers are on the assignment to destroy you. This is for those who believe that there is a word from God for your situation.

I come with that word! God is going to show your enemies that He is with you; that He will not forsake you and that you will never be defeated in Jesus' name. The enemies are going to see it and ask among themselves, "Where did mud come from?" They will say, "But there is no mud in the path of the Israelites."

This is how God will let them admit that He is with you and that He is fighting against your enemies. They said to each other, "Let us flee from the face of Israel for the Lord fighteth for them and is fighting against us."

God says to tell you, "Trouble is upon your enemies! Trouble is in the enemies' camp!" All this is taking place at the fourth watch. So, my brothers and sisters in Christ, when you are through praying and crying in the fourth watch, go to sleep. When you begin to snore and have sweet sleep, your enemies will get no sleep. "They shall have no rest," says the Lord.

God says, after you have prayed at the fourth watch, go to your bed because your prayers have released your angels to do warfare on your behalf. Your angel shall slow down your enemies with insomnia.

God says to tell you that at the fourth watch, something is taking place. At the fourth watch, the angel that God has assigned to you is gone before you to prepare a table for you right in the presence of your enemies.

The angel that God has assigned to you at the fourth watch has gone to your enemies' houses to fight them in their dreams. They will see themselves being chased by dogs and bitten by snakes.

God says to tell you that if you will get up and pray at the fourth watch of the night, a mighty turnaround is coming to your situation.

Throw your head back and declare it over your life. Speak it over your situation. I say at the fourth watch something is about to shift! Get ready for the fourth watch turnaround!

At the fourth watch your miracle becomes possible. I wonder what time it is now! It might be 3, 4, or 5 a.m. It doesn't matter, as long as you are in the fourth watch.

Guess what? In the fourth watch you only have three hours before daybreak. So, handle your business! Your prayers cannot be flat at the fourth watch. You must be intentional, because something is about to happen and it must take place before daybreak.

I want you to know that every 3 to 6 a.m. something is flowing in the spirit realm.

Whenever trouble comes your way, if you ever meet the watchers; your breakthrough is imminent. I feel a running! I feel a running! Your enemies are too close to you. Get up and pray this fourth watch warfare prayer.

Lift your right hand in the air and repeat after your teaching priest.

## Prayer

*Father please, let Your angel be a pillar of fire and a pillar of cloud.*
*Let Your angels stand between me and my enemies.*
*Never let my enemies come too close to me.*
*Come on, now speak to your angel.*
*My fourth watch warring angel, please go forth.*
*Tear the wheels off their chariots.*
*Please go forth! Go forth!*
*Jesus You are my battle axe.*
*You are my weapon of war.*

*Angels please, go forth!*
*Make a distinction between my enemies and me.*
*Draw a clear line of demarcation.*
*I am over here Lord;*
*Drive the enemies over there.*
*Lord, I see them today and they are fierce.*
*Wipe them out Lord, drown them in their fears.*
*So, I will see them again, no more, forever.*
*As You did for Your children then,*
*Do it for me today in Jesus' name.*
*Father, I give You all the glory, honour and praise*
*due unto You.*
*Thank You, Jesus, for the victory in Jesus' name.*
*Amen.*

# Chapter 11

# The Fourth Watch of The Night

Wrestling For Your Blessing

**Genesis 32**

*1 And Jacob went on his way, and the angels of God met him.*

*2 And when Jacob saw them, he said, This is God's host: and he called the name of that place Mahanaim.*

*3 And Jacob sent messengers before him to Esau his brother unto the land of Seir, the country of Edom.*

*4 And he commanded them, saying, Thus shall ye speak unto my lord Esau; Thy servant Jacob saith thus, I have sojourned with Laban, and stayed there until now:*

*5 And I have oxen, and asses, flocks, and menservants, and womenservants: and I have sent to tell my lord, that I may find grace in thy sight.*

*6 And the messengers returned to Jacob, saying, We came to thy brother Esau, and also he cometh to meet thee, and four hundred men with him.*

*7 Then Jacob was greatly afraid and distressed: and he divided the people that was with him, and the flocks, and herds, and the camels, into two bands;*

*8 And said, If Esau come to the one company, and smite it, then the other company which is left shall escape.*

*9 And Jacob said, O God of my father Abraham, and God of my father Isaac, the Lord which saidst unto me, Return unto thy country, and to thy kindred, and I will deal well with thee:*

*10 I am not worthy of the least of all the mercies, and of all the truth, which thou hast shewed unto thy servant; for with my staff I passed over this Jordan; and now I am become two bands.*

*11 Deliver me, I pray thee, from the hand of my brother, from the hand of Esau: for I fear him, lest he will come and smite me, and the mother with the children.*

*12 And thou saidst, I will surely do thee good, and make thy seed as the sand of the sea, which cannot be numbered for multitude.*

*13 And he lodged there that same night; and took of that which came to his hand a present for Esau his brother;*

*14 Two hundred she goats, and twenty he goats, two hundred ewes, and twenty rams,*

*15 Thirty milch camels with their colts, forty kine, and ten bulls, twenty she asses, and ten foals.*

*16 And he delivered them into the hand of his servants, every drove by themselves; and said unto his servants, Pass over before me, and put a space betwixt drove and drove.*

*17 And he commanded the foremost, saying, When Esau my brother meeteth thee, and asketh thee, saying, Whose art thou? and whither goest thou? and whose are these before thee?*

*18 Then thou shalt say, They be thy servant Jacob's; it is a present sent unto my lord Esau: and, behold, also he is behind us.*

*19 And so commanded he the second, and the third, and all that followed the droves, saying, On this manner shall ye speak unto Esau, when ye find him.*

*20 And say ye moreover, Behold, thy servant Jacob is behind us. For he said, I will appease him with the present that goeth before me, and afterward I will see his face; peradventure he will accept of me.*

*21 So went the present over before him: and himself lodged that night in the company.*

*22 And he rose up that night, and took his two wives, and his two womenservants, and his eleven sons, and passed over the ford Jabbok.*

*23 And he took them, and sent them over the brook, and sent over that he had.*

*24 And Jacob was left alone; and there wrestled a man with him until the breaking of the day.*

*25 And when he saw that he prevailed not against him, he touched the hollow of his thigh; and the hollow of Jacob's thigh was out of joint, as he wrestled with him.*

*26 And he said, Let me go, for the day breaketh. And he said, I will not let thee go, except thou bless me.*

According to the Holy Scriptures, Jacob was in trouble with his twin brother, Esau. He was supposed to meet him for the first time, years after their conflict.

Esau had sworn that whenever he saw him, he was going to kill him.

If you are familiar with the story, you will recall that Jacob had to run away to escape with his life. Esau's anger was indeed justified because Rachel, their mother, had conspired with Jacob and stolen his inheritance as the firstborn. This happened when Isaac their father was old and his vision was impaired. That was Jacob's second act of trickery against Esau. Earlier he had compelled him to sell him his birthright for a bowl of red pottage.

Now, after more than twenty years in Padan-Aram with their uncle Laban, Jacob is going back to meet Esau with that death sentence on his head. Jacob knew this kind of anger was not easily abated, so he was not to play with Esau.

At the fourth watch; What time?

At the fourth watch, Jacob separated from both of his wives and the children they had borne him. He sent them over the brook and was left alone. He went to a quiet place, and while he was there, a man appeared, and they began to wrestle.

Before this divine encounter, Jacob had been praying to God for Esau's wrath to be appeased before they came face to face. Jacob realised that something was different about this man and so he held on to him.

As they wrestled, the man demanded that Jacob let go of him as daybreak approached. They might have wrestled at 3, 4, and 5 a.m., but notice that as 6 a.m. drew near, something was about to take place.

The watch began to change. A new watch was about to begin. Did you hear what the angel said to Jacob? He said, "Let me go, for the day breaketh."

Why did he say this? The angel knew that his watch had ended, and he was not authorized to remain at that place outside of his watch. He could not stay in earth outside of his watch unless he were going on assignment in a different time zone.

The earth realm has different time zones. This means that when the fourth watch is coming to an end in one time zone, it is just beginning in another. So, the angel is not necessarily leaving the earth realm. He could be shifting from one time zone to another.

This particular angel was on assignment to visit Jacob. He had three hours to work and must finish his assignment before the watch ended at daybreak.

I know that the Holy Ghost is downloading this revelation in someone's spirit because I feel a shift taking place in this individual's life. Somebody, like Jacob, is saying, "I will not let you go until you bless me."

You are long overdue! Let your angel know that he has something for you and that you need it. I need my breakthrough! I need my deliverance! I need my blessing! I will not let you go until you bless me.

Come on warrior! Wrestle for your blessing! Desperate times call for desperate measures. Don't let go! Don't let go! Wrestle! Wrestle! It's almost daybreak! You have been delayed but be determined that you won't be denied in this season. It's now or never! Wrestle!

My God! I don't know about you, but I feel Him in my hands! I feel Him in my feet! I feel the power of the Holy Ghost stretching out in me. Come on believers! Connect and collect your blessing!

It's the fourth and final watch of the night. You better get radical! I am holding on to my angel. What are you going to do? Let him know that he is not going up with your blessing. He is not leaving until you get what is yours.

I feel a pull in my spirit! You do not have to remain sick. You do not have to stay bound. You do not have to remain in poverty. There is a commanded blessing with your name and address on it! A blessing is coming in the fourth watch of the night when your entire neighbourhood is asleep. You must be up wrestling and get radical with your angel to receive it.

For over five years, I have been unable to sleep until after 6 a.m. I always wondered why. I often asked, "Lord, why do I get in from church at 4 a.m. or later, tired but cannot sleep?"

At the fourth watch, sleep eludes me, and it is not a case of insomnia. Sometimes, I just lay on the bed, with my head held back. I would begin to see various persons in my spirit for whom I pray. Sometimes, I see faces that I am unable to recognize. But I still pray; I say, "Lord, I don't know this person, but as You have laid it on my heart to pray, I present him or her before You. Please intervene in this person's affairs".

Lord, I do not know what this one is going through, but Lord, I place him or her before You. There is a voice note on my phone; Lord I do not know this individual, but distance is no barrier for You. Lord, please visit this one.

There is such beauty in praying at the fourth watch. Whenever your eyes are closed, in the blink of an eye, a turnaround could take place. There is no attack that the enemy puts on you that you cannot get delivered from. You only need to know the secret.

The secret is to get up at the fourth watch and pray. Ask the Lord for that angel that has been assigned to you. Say, "Please Lord, that blessing that my angel takes to earth; please do not let him return with it. I need my blessing! I need my miracle!"

Do you agree that there is a miracle in the room with your name on it? If you do, be determined that you are not waiting for another visitation. Your angel is there with your blessing, and you want it right now! Be intentional! Say, "I am taking it in this fourth and final watch of this night."

I used to wonder about this because some time ago, the Lord told me that when He sends His angels, if a minute passes after they are to report in heaven, they cannot go back. That explains why the angel insisted that Jacob release him as the day was about to break. His shift was about to end, so it was time for him to go.

In such a situation, if you ever held on to your angel long enough and wrestled hard enough, he must release your blessing. I know that wrestling can be intense and exhausting, but be determined. Say, "I will not let you go until you bless me." If you end up with a limp, keep wrestling until you receive your blessing.

I have a rhema word for somebody going through a rough time. You have cried through the first three watches of the night. Now, God says that weeping may endure for a night, but! but! but! joy is coming at the break of the day because you wrestled in the fourth watch. Your turnaround is inevitable.

Where are the fourth watch warriors who believe a turnaround is happening right now? God is taking that weeping away and giving you joy. He is taking that mourning away and giving you dancing. Is there anyone who is determined to take it by force? The devil is a liar! Let him know, Devil, it is mine, and I am taking it tonight. My name is on it, and I am not leaving it.

I am not going to die before my time. Esau cannot kill me because God declared that I shall live and not die. Come on and release that blessing on me! Are you ready for your blessing?

If that is you, go ahead and take it! Use the weapon of worship; use the weapon of praise and pull it to you. I say, pull it to you! Pull it to you! Come on, pull it to you! pull it to you! As the praises go up, your blessings will come down. Hallelujah!

Why is it so important for me to get up and do warfare in this watch, Apostle? Because it is at this watch that some of the warring angels go to work. The Egyptians confessed, "Let us leave these people alone because it is evident that God is fighting for them."

Do you feel alone? Stop worrying about no one being in your corner. An angel is fighting for you. Don't be too lazy! Come out of the flesh! Get up at 3 a.m. and begin to war for your breakthrough. War for your deliverance! War for your miracle! War for your children! Are you ready for war? Is that warring anointing on you?

Warrior! Throw your head back, open your mouth, and shout, WARRRRRR!!!!! Go ahead and shout it! Shout it!

Shout WARRRRRR!!!!! Release a war cry! Release a war cry! Come on warrior! Release a war cry! Seh, "Mi cum yah fi tek eh, an mi nah guh weh lef eh; mi cum yah fi tek eh by force! By force mi a tek eh!"

This means war! War! War!

Shout and take it! Shout and take it! Shout and take it!

The devil is a liar! It is the fourth watch! It is now or never! I say, it is now or never! Get up! Take your healing! Get up!

Don't be afraid! Open your mouth and shout! Open your mouth and shout! Begin to make a vow to God.

**Lord, I will get up at the fourth watch and wrestle for my blessing. Lord at whatever hour you nudge me, I will obey your prompting to pray.**

**Whether 3, 4, or 5 a.m. Lord, I will pray my blessing down. I will pray until I receive my breakthrough.**

Get off the phone with people! Get in your prayer closet and talk to God. Get off Facebook! Get on your knees in intercession. Get off TikTok! Begin to worship God. God will reward you if you pray at the fourth watch.

Lift your hands and begin to praise God for what He is about to do for you because you obeyed Him in the fourth watch.

# Chapter 12

## It's Five O'clock

There are three levels of anointing in which a believer can walk. The first is an anointing that comes upon you when you are grafted into Christ. This first level of grace is described in **Titus 2:11-12**

*For the grace of God that bringeth salvation, hath appeared to all men,*
*Teaching us that, denying ungodliness and worldly lusts, we should live soberly, righteously, and godly, in this present world.*

Secondly, there is a grace or anointing that comes upon a believer by reason of the office that one occupies. God calls you, mantles you, and gives you an office. There is a grace that comes with that office. That believer will have an unction to function as a pastor, teacher, prophet, evangelist, or apostle.

But there is a third level of the anointing. It is the grace that one receives as a result of properly discerning what the Spirit of the Lord is doing in each season.

This has nothing to do with how long you have been a believer. Nor how long you have been occupying a ministerial office. You can be a believer in right standing with God and not be able to discern what God is doing in this season.

You can be effective in the area of ministry to which you have been called and do not have this third level of anointing, which means that you can preach the word of God because you were called to preach. However, you may not be relevant in a particular season.

This is not suggesting that you have backslidden, but that you either lack understanding of what God is doing in this season, or you refuse to align yourself with His current move.

Of importance is the fact that God is not using you today because He used you yesterday. The continuation of being in God's programme is dependent on many factors. Among them are hunger, pursuit and discernment of when times and seasons change and knowledge of what He is doing presently.

Whenever a season changes, it causes inconveniences. By nature, we are reluctant to make the kinds of adjustments that the new season demands. Generally speaking, people are reluctant and resistant to change.

Many still have their tents pitched in the old season and are unable to receive the new wine, the new grace for the new move. Not so with the sons of Issachar.

The Bible says that they had the ability to discern seasons. They knew what to do in each season. For this reason, they were placed in command. Everybody had to await their instructions. They were in command of giving directions because Israel had grown to trust their ability to discern the times and seasons.

So, firstly, the sons of Issachar were full of discernment through understanding. They were a people of superior understanding. They had the faculty and fortitude to discern. Discernment is a high quality of spiritual perception. The ability to perceive the impulse of the spirit. It is being able to tap into high levels of frequencies in the spirit realm that are out of the reach of others.

Secondly, the sons of Issachar had the strategy for successfully navigating the new season. In this kingdom, we win by strategy. It is good to know what worked then, but it is far more important to know what strategy must be implemented now.

The third noticeable characteristic of the sons of Issachar was their dominion in leadership. This means that they were always placed at the head because of their abilities to strategize and give solutions.

The other tribes in Israel had to wait for the sons of Issachar to take the lead while they followed. If anyone wants to be like the sons of Issachar, they will need discernment through understanding and strategies for the new season.

Hear me now! Not because this book is open, means that it is open to you. The Bible is open for you to read but God must unlock the many hidden mysteries in it for you to understand.

The Psalmist David prayed in **Psalm 119:18**

*Open thou mine eyes, that I may behold wondrous things out of Thy law.*

The day that God opens your eyes, your understanding will be activated. You will open the Holy Bible, and it will not be just a story, instead you will be reading about yourself.

Understanding is the faculty of comprehension.

**Proverbs 4:7** says:

*Wisdom is the principal thing, therefore get wisdom; and in all thy getting, get understanding.*

**Colossians 1:9**

*For this cause we also, since the day we heard it, do not cease to pray for you, and to desire that ye might be filled with the knowledge of His will in all wisdom and spiritual understanding.*

Paul prayed and desired that the believers would increase in two dimensions of knowledge. That they might be filled with the knowledge of His will in all wisdom and that they might be filled with the knowledge of His will in spiritual understanding.

A crucial aspect of spiritual understanding is the ability to understand scriptures. The ability to unlock the codes within the word of God.

Now listen to me! This understanding is an impartation that comes from God. **Luke 24:45** tells how it is achieved.

*And He opened their understanding, that they might understand the scriptures*

Other aspects of spiritual understanding include the ability to understand life. The ability to understand men. The ability to understand systems. All this is a miracle!

There is no volume of theological studies that can allow you to attain this level of understanding. It is an impartation. It is a grace that God gives to men.

No concordance, Bible dictionary, or lexicon can give spiritual understanding. There is a limit to any type of theological training one receives. However, there is no limit to spiritual understanding, which is given by the grace of God.

Spiritual understanding allows you to see what men are now looking at. This level of understanding enables you to read the handwriting on the wall.

In Daniel Chapter Five, some thought the writing on the wall was gibberish, while others saw it as a strange phenomenon. However, spiritual understanding in Daniel saw a message from God to be decoded.

Whenever understanding comes upon you, you will open your Bible and read one verse for an entire month and not be through receiving revelations.

Since the thirty-first of December Two Thousand and Twenty-Four, God has been releasing revelations of one word- GRACE- For the entire year of Two Thousand and Twenty-Five, there are truths to be unearthed from God about GRACE.

There are so many revelations. There are countless messages. There are many songs. There are poems and there are various books. Yet, GRACE will not be exhausted. That is the power of understanding.

This causes you to wonder why people use the word 'understanding' so loosely. The next time you speak to someone about 'understanding', let them know that understanding is a miracle!

There was a boy named Solomon. My God! He wrote so much about understanding. However, I want you to realize that he too, was a man of understanding.

**1Kings 3:4-15**

*4 And the king went to Gibeon to sacrifice there; for that was the great high place: a thousand burnt offerings did Solomon offer upon that altar.*

*5 In Gibeon the Lord appeared to Solomon in a dream by night and God said, Ask what I shall give thee.*

*6 And Solomon said, Thou hast shewed unto Thy servant David my father great mercy, according as he walked before Thee in truth, and in righteousness, and in uprightness of heart with Thee; and Thou has kept for him this great kindness, that Thou hast given him a son to sit on his throne, as it is this day.*

*7 And now, O Lord my God, Thou hast made Thy servant king instead of David my father: and I am but a little child: I know not how to go out or come in.*

*8 And Thy servant is in the midst of Thy people which Thou hast chosen, a great people, that cannot be numbered nor counted for multitude.*

*9 Give therefore Thy servant an UNDERSTANDING HEART to judge Thy people, that I may DISCERN between good and bad: for who is able to judge this Thy so great a people?*

*10 And the speech pleased the Lord, that Solomon had asked this thing.*

*11 And God said unto him, Because thou hast asked this thing, and hast not asked for thyself long life; neither hast asked riches for thyself, nor hast asked the life of thine enemies; but hast asked for thyself UNDERSTANDING TO DISCERN JUDGMENT,*

*12 Behold, I have done according to thy words: lo, I have given thee a WISE and an UNDERSTANDING heart; so that there was none like thee before thee, neither after thee shall any rise like unto thee.*

*13 And I have also given thee that which thou hast not asked, both riches, and honour: so that there shall not be any among the kings like unto thee all thy days.*

*14 And if thou wilt walk in My ways, to keep My statutes and My commandments, as thy father David did walk, then will I lengthen thy days.*

*15 And Solomon awoke; and, behold, it was a dream. And he came to Jerusalem, and stood before the ark of the covenant of the Lord, and offered up burnt offerings, and offered peace offerings, and made a feast to all his servants.*

Solomon's sacrifice caught God's attention and when asked what he wanted, Solomon asked for an understanding heart. It was to God a very simple request, but for Solomon, it was a big thing. Solomon was asking God for the keys.

He was indirectly saying, "Lord, you do not need to open the doors for me; just give me the keys."

Ministry is a door; it has a lock that has a code. Give me the key. Influence is a treasure chest with a code. Give me the key. Men are mysterious and complicated. Give me the key to unlock men.

Solomon's request should be the request of everyone who desires to experience the third dimension of God's grace. Who taught Solomon this? Who prepared him for God's visitation?

What wisdom! Solomon did not ask for the lives of his enemies. He understood that his enemies' death would not guarantee help from his friends. No! No! No! Do not get it twisted; enemies are not the only dangerous people.

Solomon understood that every treasure in the kingdom had gates that enclosed them. He said, I am not asking for much, but I am asking for something very important. I do not need money. I do not need vehicles. I do not need houses and lands. Solomon never even asked for anointing. He just needed the key.

To this request, God said, "You got it!" Additionally, God said, "I am giving you what you did not ask for. Riches, wealth, and honour, like no man has ever had before."

If you fast and pray for understanding, you are praying one of the most powerful prayers. Understanding is that powerful. Understanding is not just knowing how to speak. It is also knowing when to speak.

Hear me! I will repeat - life is a code. Ministry is a code; influence is a code and mankind is a code. Listen to me! There is something that you need to know about mankind. There is something that you need to know about ministry. There is something that you need to know about wealth and prosperity. There is something that you must know about the anointing. There is something that you need to know about longevity. There is something that you must know about grace. There is something that you must know about being a voice. There is something that you must know about trans-generational relevance. There is something that you must know about the hearts of men.

The miracle or the key to all mentioned above is understanding. When I received this key, I was determined not to chase money, influence, or power. No! I will just stay with understanding and watch the miracles of divine providence.

God opened my faculty to understanding. He opened my faculty to comprehend spiritual things. This was what I hungered and thirsted for, and I did not even realize that it was a desire for great grace.

No! Not until God opened my eyes and gave me the spirit of understanding.

### *The entrance of Thy word giveth light and then it gives understanding.* Psalm 119:130

I say this with humility, Jesus took me to heaven. There, He placed the entire Bible inside of me. I did not realise at the time, that what He really gave me was understanding. I was not a recipient because I was learnt but because I was hungry.

As the Lord opened my understanding about this season, I was led to revisit the history of the Apostolic faith. I was led to make a comparison of the various eras of the ministry with the manifestations of the third, sixth, ninth, and eleventh hours. These I elaborated on in previous chapters.

It is important to note that I did not revisit the first hour and you might understand why. The first hour cannot be duplicated because the Church has only one foundation. He is Jesus Christ, our Lord. In the first hour, He recruited the elders, the twelve apostles. They remain great pillars of faith in the Apostolic movement, and we continue in their doctrine as the twenty-first century church.

However, the third hour outpouring has similarities with the rebirth of the Apostolic moment in the Azusa Street Revival. This was a major outpouring of the Holy Spirit, which is considered the greatest end time revival, since Pentecost.

In Nineteen Hundred and Three, a woman who was hungry for God began to pray and she was baptised with the Holy Ghost and fire. By Nineteen Hundred and Six something began that lasted three years instead of three days. It became known as the Azusa Street Revival.

The Azusa Street Revival was a series of Pentecostal meetings that took place in Los Angeles, California at the beginning of the twentieth century. Its effects lasted ten years, from nineteen hundred and six to nineteen hundred and fifteen.

It is said that the revival began as a Bible Study conducted by William J. Seymour. He was invited to preach at a church in Los Angeles, California in the United Stares of America. However, he was later barred from doing so, because the elders disagreed with his message.

Nevertheless, with the word in him like fire, he started conducting Bible studies in one of the church member's homes. There, like the day of Pentecost, a mighty outpouring of the Holy Spirit fell on those gathered in the room.

Filled with the Holy Ghost and fire, they spoke in unknown tongues as the Spirit gave them utterance. Miracles, signs and wonders drew thousands of people from across the world to the Azusa Street Revival. As with the day of Pentecost, it also drew critics, who described the behaviour of the Christians as unorthodox.

The Azusa Street Revival brought many denominations into existence. Among them was the rebirth of the Apostolic Church, which began on the day of Pentecost.

In Nineteen Hundred and Eighteen, the Apostolic Church came to Jamaica from the United States of America through Madam Sappleton. Its first convert was a Baptist Minister named Brother Lee, who received the gospel and was filled with the Holy Ghost.

In Nineteen Hundred and Nineteen, the Pentecostal flames from the Azusa Street Revival hit Jamaica and began burning in Browns Town, St. Ann. Madam Sappleton returned to the United States and shared the good news with Elder Arthur Watson from Canada. In Nineteen Hundred and Nineteen, he came to Jamaica and met Elder Henry Lee. At that time, Elder Lee was in charge of the Pentecostal Assemblies of the World.

From this platform, Elder Watson shared the gospel of Jesus Christ. Many referred to it as the 'Oneness Jesus Name Message'. But it was powerful! It was timely and riveting! Many were converted as at the sixth hour of the day when the woman of Samaria introduced the Samaritans to Jesus.

As with the Woman at the Well in scriptures, at noon, the gospel which Madam Sappleton took to Jamaica, spread like wildfire. A revival broke out and the Apostolic Church began to take over the length and breadth of our beloved island, Jamaica.

Eighty-two souls were said to have been baptised in the name of Jesus at the first baptism. This included the first convert, Elder Lee. Twenty-five souls took on the name of Jesus in the second baptism. Among them, Melvina Whyte, founder of Emmanuel Apostolic.

Apostolicism was in Jamaica to stay. Since then, Pentecostalism in Jamaica has seen the establishment of several denominations under the Jamaica Pentecostal Union. The Apostolic Ark Pentecostal Church, Holiness Born Again Church, United Pentecostal Church and Shiloh Apostolic Church are among the earliest ones.

Over one hundred souls received baptism in the Holy Ghost weekly as these believers evangelised the island of Jamaica.

Among those heroes of the Apostolic Church in the midday outpouring was Bishop David Gallimore.

In Nineteen Hundred and Forty and the years immediately following, another wind blew as at the ninth hour. In this outpouring, God used another set of men and women, as He used Peter and John, to fan the revival flames with a powerful delivery of the word, confirmed with miracles, signs, and wonders.+

Bishop Ivan Evans, Bishop Zachariah Nepaul, and Bishop John Watson were among the ninth-hour stalwarts, through whom God's mighty power was manifested in the Apostolic church during that era.

Today, I feel humbled and privileged to be a part of the final hour of Apostolic believers. We are the five o'clock set. This is the final hour, and God is doing a new thing. In this season, God is combining the manifestations of the third, sixth, and ninth hours into a great final-hour outpouring on this generation.

While some are trying to divide and create segregation through wars among us, others are so hungry for the former and the latter rain. These are watchers who are in earnest prayers and fasting, hungry for the new move of God.

God is about to pour His Spirit upon this world again. God is raising up preachers who will declare the One God Apostolic gospel, without compromise. These end time warriors are not afraid to say that Jesus is God! There is no fear of rejection or ridicule, when declaring that Jesus is the only way.

They preach in and out of season that Jesus is the Father in creation, the Son in redemption, and the Holy Ghost in the Church. They stand on the word of God, that baptism must be done in Jesus' name and that without the Holy Ghost, we are none of His. They continue to spread the Apostles' doctrine that we need to be filled with the Holy Ghost with the initial evidence of speaking in unknown tongues.

Praise God! King Jesus Pentecostal Fellowship is privileged to be a part of the five o'clock crew. This move of God began at a church sister's family dinner table in Havendale, Kingston, Jamaica in Two Thousand Six. It continued as a weekly prayer meeting at that same house, until Two Thousand and Seven, when it moved to the Medallion Hall Hotel, also in Kingston.

This move was inevitable, as the house could no longer accommodate the growing crowd. In the meantime, God was training His servant at the backside of the desert in Hide Away Lane, Negril, Westmoreland.

All these experiences led to the birth of King Jesus Pentecostal Fellowship in Two Thousand and Twelve.

The first branch in western Jamaica started on the highway to Negril. Nompriel Road, Sheffield, Westmoreland to be more specific.

The headquarters in Kingston moved from the house in Havendale, to the Medallion Hall hotel, then to Patrick Gardens Community Centre, still in Kingston.

The ministry grew and so too did great opposition from some members of the community. They complained that the church was too noisy and that the heavy flow of traffic was inconveniencing them and restricting their access to and from their homes.

All this was just a setup for the greatest move in the ministry at the time of writing this book. The church was served an eviction notice. Praise be to the Most High God! The closed door to Patrick Gardens Community Centre opened a huge door at 138-140 Red Hills Road, Kingston.

We were overflowing at the previous location to accommodate a few hundred worshippers. Now, in 2025, a little over two years after arriving at our present location, we are once again overflowing – our Sunday services are usually jam-packed.

If this is not a revival, I wonder what is. But God said to me, "Son, you have not seen anything as yet!" The Apostolic faith is strengthening, reuniting and in the initial stages of what I believe is going to be the greatest move of God in the earth before the rapture.

The miracles are too many to mention in this book. You will be privileged to hear some of the testimonies of those who experienced miracles, signs and wonders in a subsequent release, titled 'The Book of Testimonies'.

God told me that the year 2025 represents Five o'clock in the realm of the spirit. This season, great grace is being released in the earth at this final hour. This mighty move of God, the eleventh and final-hour outpouring, will be reaping the end-time harvest in earnest.

God continues to move by His Spirit. Persons are being baptized in the name of Jesus Christ and being filled with the Holy Ghost in astonishing numbers.

Not only that, but the ministry has gone global by the great grace of our Lord and Saviour, Jesus Christ. There are now nineteen churches in five countries across the globe.

Let somebody know that the revival continues. Azusa Street is repeating itself. I do not know about you, but I know that God is moving. I do not know what you believe, but I am sure that God is saving to the utmost, and He is adding to the church daily, such as should be saved.

I praise Him as I think about King Jesus Pentecostal Fellowship's growth and brief history. I look with admiration on the rapid growth and maturity in Kingston. As I reminisce, I just say, Lord! Thank You!

See, whenever a preacher is called by God and continues to preach; when he knows that he is one who God calls, He will feed the church of God. He will nourish the body of Christ. He preaches until some are vexed, and some do not admire him anymore.

A preacher who is consistent in preaching will experience personal growth and growth in ministry. Growth is not measured only by numbers. Sometimes, church growth is measured by the stability that believers who once struggled, achieve.

There were times when those who are now passionately evangelizing once asked themselves, "Am I in the right church? Is this where I am supposed to be at this time?"

Some wondered if they were serving the right God. Others were not sure if Jesus was indeed God. Some were confused about observing laws and ordinances that have been fulfilled by Jesus. As you continue to feed them with the word of God, they become established in the faith.

I recall those days when the babes in the ministry at Kingston would say that they needed real fire. They travelled in large numbers to attend services in Negril because the fire blazed there. But today, I sit and observe the service in Kingston, and praise God for the fire which now blazes there.

My heart is greatly encouraged. It has proven to me when my work is not in vain in the Lord. I realize that there is a wildfire burning, it is now blazing in Negril, at the western end of the island of Jamaica, and red hot in Kingston, the eastern end of the island.

Seeing persons willing to be baptized in the name of Jesus Christ at every service is a catalyst for me. It energizes my spirit and pushes me to go on. I am here to boldly declare that I am not tired yet!

If you are a real warrior, with a passion to see souls added to the kingdom daily, shout, I am not tired yet! I admire the Men's Choir in our Negril branch. In a time when men are seen as weak and soft if they surrender their lives to Jesus, here a set of real men with the majority in their twenties and early thirties are ablaze for Jesus. Sons of God, remain on fire for Jesus. Do not let anyone discourage you. Do not allow anybody to steal your joy, your praise, or your worship.

Having become rooted and grounded, they are now ready to run with the gospel. There is a zeal to take the truth to the byways and hedges at this final hour of the harvest. The Pentecostal fire is burning among us. I hear the sound of an abundance of rain. Many have been desperate to see the move of God again in the earth.

**Romans 8:19** *For the earnest expectation of the creature waiteth for the manifestation of the sons of God.*

The time is here! The time is now! You are at the right place and at the right time to experience the former and latter rain outpouring. You are at the right place, at the right time to experience great grace. You can have it if you are hungry enough.

# Chapter 13

# The Hour of Great Grace

The word grace is not used as frequently in the Old Testament as in the New Testament. However, grace was evident in both dispensations.

God's grace was constantly extended to the Israelites, His chosen people, while they walked in the old covenant. It is expressed extensively throughout the writing of the new covenant, called the dispensation of grace.

Speaking of dispensations, I am led to give you a synopsis of the dispensations from creation to present, to create a backdrop for the word I am about to release from the Lord for this season.

There is the dispensation of innocence. This is from creation to the fall of man. This is so called because in the physical realm, Adam was not aware of the fact that he was not wearing physical clothing. At this point, all things were pure before him.

Following the fall, the dispensation of conscience came into existence. This existed from the fall to the flood. There were no laws or rules. Man simply functioned according to his conscience, self-ruled in this dispensation, and did as their conscience dictated.

God concluded that every imagination of the heart of men was evil continually.

This is what happens when we are estranged from God and enveloped in ourselves. Unchecked, this situation gets worse; hence, from time to time, God raises up a voice of reason.

A voice that fearlessly blows the trumpet, echoing that there is a God and that He must be obeyed for a nation to prosper. A voice that reminds mankind that there are principles, rules, and regulations that the Creator has established. These are in place to make us aware that flesh, self, and conscience will only lead us farther and farther away from God. Eventually, God will have to judge such a nation.

Where there is no theology, there is no rule. Where there is no God, the heart of man becomes increasingly deceitful and desperately wicked. Mankind became so ruthless that it repented God that He made man. You will remember that God made man in His likeness and in His image. Yet, in the dispensation of conscience, man wanted to exist in their likeness and image.

The entrance of Noah ended the era of consciousness. He sailed from the shores of consciousness into the safety of Mount Ararat and landed in the third dispensation. This was the dispensation of human government. It existed from Noah to Abraham; during which time there were patriarchs who established rules and reigns.

As Abraham came on the scene, a new dispensation emerged. This was the dispensation of promise. You see, God gave Abraham a promise to which he clung, and it changed the entire trajectory of his life. This era lasted until Moses graced the stage.

Moses introduced the dispensation of law, which lasted until Jesus Christ. The law of God was given and with that came theocracy. So, from Mount Sinai to Mount Calvary was the dispensation of law.

At that juncture, the dispensation in which we now live began. This is the dispensation of grace. It spans from the day of Pentecost to the rapturing of the church.

The biblical concept of grace refers to the free, unmerited, or undeserved favour of God. However, the application of grace to any situation results in a 'BUT GOD' experience. So, for me, grace simplified is 'BUT GOD!'

### Genesis 6:1-8
*And it came to pass, when men began to multiply on the face of the earth, and daughters were born unto them,*

*2 That the sons of God saw the daughters of men that they were fair; and they took them wives of all which they chose.*

*3 And the Lord said, My spirit shall not always strive with man, for that he also is flesh: yet his days shall be an hundred and twenty years.*

*4 There were giants in the earth in those days; and also after that, when the sons of God came in unto the daughters of men, and they bare children to them, the same became mighty men which were of old, men of renown.*

*5 And God saw that the wickedness of man was great in the earth, and that every imagination of the thoughts of his heart was only evil continually.*

*6 And it repented the Lord that He had made man on the earth, and it grieved Him at His heart.*

*7 And the Lord said, I will destroy man whom I have created from the face of the earth; both man, and beast, and the creeping thing, and the fowls of the air; for it repenteth Me that I have made them.*

*8 But Noah found grace in the eyes of the Lord.*

You will recall that Noah lived in the dispensation of conscience. God was grieved by mankind's behaviour. Like today, men had become very wicked. They believed that they had the right to kill whomever they wanted to and to place witchcraft on whomever they wanted to.

If someone stepped on another's toe, a visit would be made to the obeahman, and payment would be made to destroy that person's family. Evil altars would be erected to fight against the prosperity of a neighbour.

Men were having intimate affairs with men, ignoring the laws of nature and of God. Everyone did whatever they pleased with no regard for their Creator.

God said, "You believe that you are in charge because you live according to your good pleasure. You consider yourselves to be independent of Me; capable of surviving on your own. Watch out!" That is what God was referring to when He said that His Spirit does not always strive with man.

The word 'strive' is derived from a Hebrew word which means 'to plea, to knock, to beg'. God was saying that His Spirit will not always nudge or convict you.

Let me break this down with an example. The Holy Ghost would prick your heart if you came to church today and received the Holy Ghost but after leaving church you went and stole. This initial conviction will be so strong that you would break down in tears and return the stolen item.

This happens because of the intensity of God's pleading or striving with you. However, should you repeat the same sinful practice tomorrow, God's conviction will not come to you with the same forcefulness or intensity.

While He continues to knock, the conviction becomes weaker and weaker. Eventually, you no longer feel any remorse about stealing and continue the sinful practice without feeling convicted.

God has stopped striving with you because of your rebellion. The Spirit of God has left that area of your life. Your conscience now becomes seared with a hot iron.

That is why it is so important for persons with the Holy Ghost not to play with their salvation. I know that piece is hard, and somebody's heart is beating fast. But stay with me and take heed! The truth will set you free.

God decided to place a limit on man in this dispensation because of their wickedness. They were accustomed to living for over nine hundred years. However, because of their evil practices, God reduced their lifespan to one hundred and twenty years.

Why did God cut their lifespan so short? Just imagine if any of the renowned gang leaders of our day were allowed to live for nine hundred years. Can you imagine the level of wickedness that they would unleash on our society?

Not only that! They would be recruiting others to expand their criminal network. Before you knew it, as God said of those in Noah's time, "evil would continually be in their hearts." Evil people, left unchecked, become so crafty and dangerous that they can destroy any nation and eventually the world.

God says that even when you feel large and untouchable and that no one can talk to you, He will put a time on you. And should the need arise, He will cut you off without remedy.

Today, God is knocking again. Do not harden your heart. Do not stiffen your neck. Remember that He will not always strive with you. He will not always knock on your heart or plead with you. Answer the call! Answer the call!

In recent times, we have seen a similar occurrence in some countries, as we saw in the dispensation of conscience. Everyone is free to choose what they want to do and who or what they want to be. Flags are being placed on prominent buildings, declaring to the world that they endorse and take pride in the things that God calls abominable.

The movie series, including cartoons, now portray homosexuality and lesbianism as the norm. Same-sex marriages and families are being promoted as being acceptable. The education system in many areas of the world is being overhauled to remove the Bible from schools and introduce literature that teaches, in various ways, that homosexuality and lesbianism are a new norm.

People- including children- are free to choose what they want to be identified as, including animals. I know that this can be a provocative conversation for one who is involved in an alternate lifestyle. The same is true for those close to someone who is involved.

Let me make this clear. I am not discriminating against sinners. In fact, we all have sinned and come short of the glory of God. I do not bash sinners; I pray for sinners to repent and turn from sin. BUT! BUT! BUT! Unapologetically, I call sin what it is: SIN.

In response to the pervasiveness of homosexuality and lesbianism, referred to as 'PRIDE'. God raised up a leader who is not a politician by nature, who is wealthy and surrounded by wealthy supporters. This means, he cannot be easily bribed. God has used him to confirm His words in **Proverbs 16:18**.

*PRIDE goeth before destruction, and a haughty spirit before a fall.*

God was so angry! Can you imagine? He was so grieved with the people in Noah's generation, that He decided to destroy everything on the face of the earth, including man, beast, and plants. Why? Because the imagination of their hearts was evil continually.

God was so grieved, that He repented doing something which He had so much pleasure in initially. At creation, the Bible says that God took a look at everything He made and saw that it was good. But now, of the same things, contaminated with evil, God says, "I am sorry that I made them."

As I reflect on this generation, I pause to pray.

## Prayer

*Lord, please continue to be my Father.*
*Correct me whenever I need correction.*
*Fix me whenever I need fixing.*
*Rebuke me when I need to be rebuked.*
*God, I'd rather that you give me a little whipping so that I can keep on ticking.*
*So, chastise me whenever I need to be chastened.*
*But please, do not regret saving me.*
*Do not regret delivering me.*
*Do not drive me out of Your presence.*
*Oh God! Please, never say that You do not want me to be Your child anymore.*
*Never be sorry that You gave me the Holy Ghost and gifts.*
*Lord, please, may You never repent that You placed this calling on my life.*
*Let me never grieve You to the point that You take my ministry.*
*Most importantly, Oh God, please do not destroy me.*
*Lord, hear my humble cry for grace and mercy in Jesus' mighty name.*
*Amen*

The entire world is heading in the same direction as the people in Noah's time. The great United States of America which once declared, 'In God we trust' is among the nations who seemingly had forgotten their God.

However, in one day, executive orders were used to veto laws which upheld ungodliness and to declare righteous laws in the land. God is looking for leaders in Two Thousand and Twenty-Five who will blow the trumpet and sound the alarm. Leaders who will turn the hearts of the people back to God.

God is looking for preachers like Noah in this dispensation. Preachers who will fearlessly preach that judgement is inevitable wherever sin is prominent. Noah preached for one hundred and twenty years, although they mocked him and refused to repent.

Can God find a preacher who will 'lik eh til eh buss'? One who will set his face like flint and declare, 'Thus saith God'? A preacher who will preach in season and out of season. A voice who will not fear, whether they want to hear or forbear. A trumpet of God who will blow real hard, unbothered by fame or popularity. A preacher who will just preach!!!!

Noah was from the dispensation of conscience, but his heart's response to God, gained him an unusual opportunity. Noah was able to tap into the realm of the spirit and step over the dispensation of law into the dispensation of grace.

**Genesis 6:8** says:

***Noah found grace in the eyes of the Lord.***

Watch this! Grace did not find Noah. Noah found grace. It was hidden from him in a distant dispensation, but gazing into the eyes of the Lord transported Noah into the unknown. God is looking for a set of people who are that eager to know their God. Are you one of them?

The year 2025 reminds me of the days of Noah. God revealed to me at the close of 2024, that the coming year would be like none we ever experienced. As we crossed over into the new season, He said, "Son you will need new strategies to navigate these waters."

God is doing something fresh, and like the sons of Issachar and Noah, you must be in sync with the Spirit of God to discern what He is doing.

There is an end-time harvest to be reaped and spoils to collect. To accomplish both requires realignment. This is a prophetic year! Five is the number of grace. It is the number of favour and it is the number of truth.

God sets man up on the number of five. Whatever you are going to touch, you need five fingers. Wherever you are going, you need five toes on each foot. This symbolizes that five is God's grace to you.

Crossing over into a new year, season, or dimension is usually a time of separation. Not only are you required to leave the old stuff behind, but some people cannot cross over with you either.

In 2024, bad mind, covetousness, hate, obeah, lack, and poverty were the companions of many believers. We tried hard to run from them, but they kept chasing after and overtaking us.

But not so in 2025 and beyond! This year, we are going to submerge ourselves under grace. In Jamaican parlance, 'A gaan duck under grace!' This simply means I am going to place myself under grace.

Bad mind is not coming with me!

Covetousness is not coming with me!

Obeah is not coming with me!

Curse is not coming with me!

This year, grace is running after you. It shall overtake you and bring you into the abundant life in Christ Jesus.

A new season is released!

A new day has dawned!

God says, "I am going to do a new thing. I am indeed angry, and judgment is about to be released."

Water was about to destroy the earth. BUT! BUT! BUT!

Let me tell you about 'BUT'. "BUT" is a conjunction used to join two or more phrases. However, 'BUT' is a contrasting conjunction. Whatever was said before 'BUT' is flipped, overturned, or vetoed after the word 'BUT' is used.

It doesn't matter what was said before; whenever 'BUT' is released, it no longer applies. In the Bible, whatever time a 'BUT' appears, anything said before that 'BUT' no longer has strength.

I do not care what negativity was released over your life; take a moment to wave your hand over your head and declare, 'There is a 'BUT' over my life today.'

Did you know that "grace" is a 'BUT GOD MOMENT'? Let me show you. Remember that Joseph was in Egypt because of his brothers' hatred and jealousy. However, in **Genesis 50:20**, Joseph said to them:

*BUT as for you, ye thought evil against me, BUT GOD meant it unto good, to bring to pass, as it is this day, to save much people alive.*

I do not care how much they hate the children of God. I do not care how much they plot, plan, or scheme against a believer; if there is a 'BUT', God will turn their evil into good.

**Matthew 19:28:**
*BUT Jesus beheld them, and said unto them, With men this is impossible: BUT with God all things are possible.*

Let somebody know that like David in **Psalm 3:2-3**:

*Many there be which say of my soul, There is no help for him in God.*
*BUT Thou, O Lord, art a shield for me; my glory, and the lifter up of mine head.*

You see, whenever you come to church, some people in your family do not expect you to come to anything in life. Their mouths are constantly on you. They look at you with scorn and say that there is no help for you in God.

Let me give you a few more powerful, life-transforming 'BUT' verses for you to declare over your life. These are demonstrations of the grace of God in the lives of God's people.

Speak them over yourself, your loved ones and in your difficult situations. Use them to encourage and strengthen your soul in the Lord. Perilous times are ahead, BUT GOD!

Paul told Timothy in **2 Timothy 1:7**

*For God has not given us the spirit of fear; BUT of power, and of love, and of a sound mind.*

Tell somebody, I used to be fearful; I once walked in dread and timidity, BUT GOD!

The devil is a liar!

Do you have a 'BUT'? If you do, open your mouth, throw your head back and shout:

**Psalm 34:10**
*The young lions do lack, and suffer hunger: BUT! they that seek the Lord shall not want any good thing.*

**Ephesians 2:12-13**
*That at that time ye were without Christ, being aliens from the commonwealth of Israel, and strangers from the covenants of promise, having no hope, and without God in the world:*
*BUT now in Christ Jesus ye who sometimes were far off are made nigh by the blood of Christ.*

### Romans 6:14
*For sin shall not have dominion over you: for ye are not under the law, BUT under grace.*

There was a time when we were under law. During this time, sin had us bound. But I can shout that I am now under grace.

### John 1:17
*For the law was given by Moses, BUT grace and truth came by Jesus Christ.*

Today is a day of 'BUT!'
This year is a year of 'BUT!'
This is a 'BUT GOD!' season.

### Matthew 19:30
*BUT many that are first shall be last, and the last shall be first.*

Right now, you might be going through some rough times. You might be facing tough decisions at this moment. Someone is currently being afflicted by the enemy. You are under pressure, BUT I want you to know this:

### Psalm 34:19
*Many are the afflictions of the righteous: BUT! the Lord delivereth him out of them all.*

### Psalm 20:7
*Some trust in chariots, and some in horses: BUT we will remember the name of the Lord our God.*

### Ephesians 5:8
*For ye were sometimes darkness, BUT now are ye light in the Lord: walk as children of light.*

Who am I talking to?

Somebody has been weeping for a long time. Come on now! Get up and speak to that thing that has had you weeping all night. Say, BUT GOD!

### Psalm 30:5
*Weeping may endure for a night BUT joy cometh in the morning.*

Repeat that several times until your tears of sorrow flee and the joy of the Lord returns. Weeping may endure for a night, BUT! A BUT is coming! A BUT is coming!

If you believe it, throw your head back and shout it one more time!

Hallelujah! This is a great time to take a praise break.

Shout! Shout it! Shout it! Shou it!

Declare it! Declare this thing!

A turnaround is about to take place!

My weeping days are about to be over!

My mourning days are about to end!

A "BUT" is coming my way!

A "BUT" is coming my way!

Shout it clear! Shout! Come on! Shout it clear!

The devil is a liar! The devil is a liar!

BUT! BUT! BUT! I don't care who is fainting around you in 2025 or whatever time you are reading this word. Hear me! I don't care who is falling in this season. God says to tell you:

**Isaiah 40:30-31**

*Even the youths shall faint and be weary, and the young men shall utterly fall:*

*BUT they that wait upon the Lord shall renew their strength; they shall mount up with wings as eagles; they shall run, and not be weary; and they shall walk, and not faint.*

Throw your head back and praise God if a BUT is in your life.

Shout! Shout! Shout!

There is a BUT!

There is a BUT!

There is a BUT!

There is a BUT!

There is a BUT!

We are in the number FIVE this season. God is doing a new thing in 2025.

**Romans 6:23**

*The wages of sin is death; BUT the gift of God is eternal life through Jesus Christ our Lord.*

Amid judgment; amid trouble; amid failure; amid disappointment, there is a BUT. God was angry and was about to destroy everything. But, in **Genesis 6:8**, the Bible says:

**BUT Noah found grace in the eyes of the Lord.**

You better open your mouth!

You better open your mouth and shout 'GREAT GRACE!'

You better open your mouth and shout 'GREAT GRACE!'

Who am I talking to? Are you searching for more grace? Is there any warrior, who, like Noah, wants something from God that is beyond the ordinary?

Great grace was hidden. Do you hear me? I said that grace was hidden from Noah's generation. They were living in the era of conscience and grace would not be coming until another four dispensations.

But Noah was able to tap out of his time. He stepped over promise; he stepped over human government; he stepped over law and walked into the grace of God.

I do not know about you, but great grace is on me today. This is a higher level of the grace that Noah found. I do not know about you, but I have found great grace. I should have been dead; I could have been dead, BUT GREAT GRACE!

If you can identify with me. Open your mouth! I say, open your mouth and shout GREAT GRACE! Open your mouth and let hell know that the great grace of God is on you right now. Let hell know that the great grace of God is around you right now. The great grace of God is upon you right now.

On numerous occasions, the devil tried to kill me, but because of God's great grace, I am here today. The devil took away my family. He attacked my finances and tried to destroy my body with sickness and diseases. He thought that after all that, I would have lost my mind. BUT GOD'S GREAT GRACE!

If you are under attack at this moment, open your mouth and drive that devil out right now. Remember that life and death are in the power of your tongue. Drive him out now and declare that by the great grace of God, I am set free. Let the devil know that you are saved by God's great grace.

You and I deserved every bit of what the devil tried to put on us, BUT GOD'S GREAT GRACE! When you say 'great grace,' demons tremble. Do not keep silent, because whenever you say 'great grace', Satan gets upset. He becomes angry, cross, and miserable.

At the mention of 'great grace', hell shakes. Declare 'great grace' and watch your mind be renewed. Echo 'great grace!' and anxiety has to flee. Shame and worry cannot stay when you mention great grace.

Get up! Walk around and shout great grace! Shout great grace!

You do not earn great grace. You do not work for great grace. You do not deserve great grace. You are not eligible for great grace. Great grace is only given by the mercy of God.

If you believe you have it, shout, 'Great grace is in my house!'

Great Grace is more than mercy; it is more than forgiveness.

One acronym describes grace as:

**G**-od's
**R**-iches
**A**-t
**C**-hrist's
**E**-xpense

When you say 'great grace' you are saying 'power'. When you say 'great grace' you are speaking of abilities. When you say 'great grace' you are talking about the unction to function.

When you say 'great grace' you are admitting that there are things that should have killed you and erased your memory from the surface of the earth, BUT GOD'S GREAT GRACE! said, "NO!"

Declare that you have great grace. I have great grace to be me. You could never be me, and I would never want to be you. I am what I am because of His great grace. I carry great grace, just to be me.

Do you have great grace? You have great grace to run your race. You have great grace to raise that boy or that girl. You have great grace to handle that child with autism or any other health issues.

You have great grace to receive that job for which you are not qualified. Great grace is on you to receive that promotion. You have great grace to marry that man or woman and maintain a healthy marriage.

There is great grace on you to manage that office or to successfully operate that business. You have great grace to fill that position. There is great grace that allows you to live in that community. Say, Great grace!

Noah found grace; it is an invisible force.

Great grace is Dunamis. That hidden gift will manifest through great grace. I've got great grace! What say you?

It matters not how old I am, I've got great grace. Regardless of how fat or skinny I am, I have great grace. As long as I have great grace, my physical appearance fades into oblivion. Great grace is what I want to be seen on me. Whether they are fond of you or not, you have great grace. Declare this: I have great grace, and there is nothing that you can do about it. You can't kill me before my time. You can't stop or hinder me. Even when you say 'death', great grace is speaking over me. Great grace says, "I shall not die but live and declare the works of God."

Whenever you say that I am finished, great grace says, "No, I am just getting ready to step into a new dimension."

You laughed because I was down, but guess what? Great grace is picking me up again.

I feel something shifting again! If you can feel the shift, then go ahead and begin to praise God for the shift that the great grace of God has brought to your life.

Noah found grace. It was hidden. It was out of his time. He transcended his era and his dispensation and moved into what was hidden, and God revealed to Noah what He was about to do. God also told Noah what he needed to do. He told him to build an ark.

Great grace will keep you building amid chaos. Great grace will continue your advancement, while all kinds of mouths are speaking ill about you. Great grace will anoint you to keep on preaching amid turmoil.

Great grace will propel you to get up and show up at that workplace that is full of witchcraft. In the midst of wars, pandemics, mass deportations, violence and threats, great grace will keep you and prosper you.

In this season where churches, including the Apostolic churches, are fighting against each other, great grace has raised up King Jesus Pentecostal Fellowship (KJPF). Right amid covetousness, hatred, and bad mind. At the end of January 2025, and for emphasis, note that this is only one month that great grace led thirty-five souls to take on the name of Jesus, by water baptism in our Negril branch and for the same period, our Kingston branch, baptized fifty-eight souls in the name of Jesus.

This is amid the turmoil when men are lovers of pleasures more than lovers of God. In an era where men are self-seeking and following their own hearts' desires.

You are not reading or listening to this by chance; great grace led you to it. You are not a part of this ministry by chance, you are on an assignment. God is about to shake the world again and has chosen you for this hour. Yes! Great grace brought you into the kingdom for such a time as this. Give God glory for His great grace!

# Chapter 14

# Collecting The Spoils

**2 Chronicles 20:20-25**

*20 And they rose early in the morning, and went forth into the wilderness of Tekoa: and as they went forth, Jehoshaphat stood and said, Hear me, O Judah, and ye inhabitants of Jerusalem; Believe in the Lord your God, so shall ye be established; believe his prophets, so shall ye prosper.*

*21 And when he had consulted with the people, he appointed singers unto the Lord, and that should praise the beauty of holiness, as they went out before the army, and to say, Praise the Lord; for his mercy endureth for ever.*

*22 And when they began to sing and to praise, the Lord set ambushments against the children of Ammon, Moab, and mount Seir, which were come against Judah; and they were smitten.*

*23 For the children of Ammon and Moab stood up against the inhabitants of mount Seir, utterly to slay and destroy them: and when they had made an end of the inhabitants of Seir, every one helped to destroy another.*

*24 And when Judah came toward the watch tower in the wilderness, they looked unto the multitude, and, behold, they were dead bodies fallen to the earth, and none escaped.*

*25 And when Jehoshaphat and his people came to take away the spoil of them, they found among them in abundance both riches with the dead bodies, and precious jewels, which they stripped off for themselves, more than they could carry away: and they were three days in gathering of the spoil, it was so much.*

This is the word God placed in my spirit to release at the Crossover Service into the year 2025.

God says to tell you that IT IS 5 P.M.! What happens at 5 p.m. Apostle? The HOUR OF GRACE! It's the hour when the first becomes the last and the last becomes the first! It's the hour of collecting the spoils!

In 2 Chronicles 20:25, Jehoshaphat and his people came to take away the spoils of those whom God killed. Yes! Sometimes, God has to cut down some so that the wealth of the wicked can be transferred to the righteous.

The Bible says that the wealth of the wicked is laid up for the just. People of God, it's time to collect the spoils! God says that this is the year that you are collecting everything.

I released this world at midnight on December thirty-first, Two Thousand and Twenty-Four, as we crossed into 'The Year of Great Grace and the Collecting of the Spoils.' Immediately after this declaration, President Trump made some major shifts in the United States of America through executive orders. Some of which confirmed that God is doing a new thing in this season.

One of the executive orders signed by the incoming president includes the reinstatement of some service members who were dismissed by the outgoing administration. They were dismissed for refusing to take the COVID-19 vaccine during the pandemic.

However, it did not stop there! They will be fully compensated for all the remuneration lost while dismissed. This is a prime example of what God is doing for His people in this hour. Yes! It will be an hour of darkness and catastrophe but amid all the chaos, great grace is going to rest upon God's people in this final hour. We are going to collect the spoils from our enemies.

God is restoring to His people what the enemy has stolen, and He is going to give us double for our trouble. God says, "I am not only reinstating you, but for all the days of hell that you have endured, you are going to be reaping the spoils in this season."

Now declare it over your life! Everything that the devil has held up for me, everything that he has stolen, all that I was deprived of as a result of COVID-19, I am recovering all in this season.

In 2025, God is going to give you back your business. He is going to restore your health. He is going to revive your ministry. It's reaping season! Lift your hands, throw your head back, and shout,

I AM HEALED!

I AM RESTORED!

I AM DELIVERED IN JESUS' NAME!

I know that you are wondering how this is going to happen because your enemies are many and they are great. In some cases, they have joined forces with other enemies to destroy you. Notice that the attack on Israel mentioned in this chapter was neither their first nor last. In a previous chapter, the attack by the Egyptians at the Red Sea was highlighted.

It is quite similar in our lives as believers. We sometimes say, "As one thing is off, another is on!" That is so true; it demonstrates the relentless nature of our adversaries. But don't worry! **Exodus 15:13** says that our God, ***The Lord is a man of war. The Lord is His name.*** This is the hour when the Lion shall come out of the Lamb and fight for His people. Fret not thyself! This battle is not yours; it is the Lord's.

We are using the same strategy that Jehoshaphat employed which gave Israel the victory described in **2 Chronicles 20:25**. Notice that this is the year we are in, and history is about to repeat itself in this hour. We are going to cry to God in prayer and then we are going to praise Him for the victory. Are you ready?

The angels are here on assignment to take your worship, mixed with your prayer to the throne room and they are coming back with your victory. It is time for war! Now is not the time to be sad or depressed; it is time to pray and worship. Get ready to give God your best praise! Get ready to cry unto Him from the depths of your spirit.

The devil does not like you, and your enemies are fighting you. Enemies want to destroy you. Your enemies are also bigger, stronger, and more powerful than you.

Whether they come against us the way that they came against Moses or like they did Jehoshaphat, the outcome will be the same. You are at the right place, and it is the right time for God to turn things around for you. I feel someone right now who is like the children of Israel. You are coming out of that bondage!

You are under pressure! Pharoah's army is behind you; mountains are on either side and the Red Sea is before you. What are you going to do? Pressure is on every side and the devil is determined that he must get you out.

What are you going to do? I am giving you the same instructions that Moses gave the children of Israel.

*STAND STILL AND SEE THE SALVATION OF THE LORD, WHICH HE WILL SHOW UNTO YOU TODAY. FOR THE EGYPTIANS WHOM YOU HAVE SEEN TODAY, YOU SHALL SEE THEM AGAIN, NOMORE FOREVER.*

If you want God to move them forever, you have to give God real praise. Some praises will move your enemies forever. These are not ordinary praises.

**Exodus 14:14** goes something like this:

*The Lord shall fight for you and you shall hold your peace.*

What are you going to do when there is trouble on every side? You cannot look behind you, because Pharoah and his army is there. You cannot look to the right or left because the mountains are too high, the Red Sea is too wide; the Red Sea is too high; the Red Sea is too deep. What are you going to do?

You have to throw your head back! You must open your mouth and praise the only wise God. The only one who can fight for you; the only one who can give you victory. The one who can heal your body and deliver you.

Open your mouth and praise God if you are under pressure right now. If you are under pressure, it is time for you to shift the dynamics with a praise.

Shift it with a praise. Some people sing because everybody is singing. Some people dance because everybody is dancing, but know this: not everybody is dancing because dancing is going on. Not everybody is singing because singing is going on.

Some people know that whenever they sing to God from the bottom of their bellies, God will show up and fix their situation. The Bible says that when you are about to enter the house of God, you should enter His gates with thanksgiving and into His courts with praise. Be thankful unto Him and bless His Holy name. This can be applied right where you are.

When all hell is breaking loose in your life, regardless of where you are, it is the best time to praise God. Moses did it! Jehoshaphat did it! They stilled the people and shifted their focus from the magnitude of their circumstances to the power and might of their God.

I am telling somebody right now. Your future is hidden in God. Your blessing is in Jesus Christ. Your healing is in His hands right now. Your breakthrough is in the hands of the Lord and you are about to collect the spoils of your enemies.

If you ever give God real praise right now, He will turn your darkness into light. He will shift your situation. Look at what Moses and Jehoshaphat did after they stilled the people. They sang praises unto God. Jehoshaphat's account is already recorded at the beginning of this chapter.

Now, listen to Moses in **Exodus 15:**

*1Then sang Moses and the children of Israel this song unto the Lord, and spake, saying, I will sing unto the Lord, for he hath triumphed gloriously: the horse and his rider hath He thrown into the sea.*

*2 The Lord is my strength and song, and He is become my salvation: He is my God, and I will prepare Him an habitation; my father's God, and I will exalt Him.*

I stop at this point to tell you, wherever you are right now; if you just stop whatever you are doing and prepare a habitation for God. If you ever begin to praise God from your spirit right now. As the praises go up, your deliverance will come down. Who am I talking to?

There was nowhere to go, nowhere to turn. But the men of God stilled the people. Do not wait until the battle is over; shout now. They sang amid the problem, and God intervened. The enemies turned on each other and destroyed themselves. All the children of Israel had to focus on was praising God and collecting the spoils from among the dead bodies of their enemies.

While Moses and the children of Israel stood at the Red Sea, the Bible says that an east wind came. It blew and blew until the Red Sea was divided. The people of God crossed over on dry land while the Egyptians drowned.

If you keep your mouth shut, you will never experience your miracle. However, if you learn to be still and know that He is God; if you ever learn to praise Him while the pain is rocking your body. If you ever learn to lift Him up; if you ever learn to give God a crazy praise. Where are the warriors?

I heard when Moses said:

### 3 The Lord is a man of war: the Lord is His name.

I come here to tell you that whenever family, witches or devils rise against you; when your friends become your enemies, if you ever learn to get into the presence of God; forget about what you are going through, open your mouth and begin to give God a crazy praise; God will go before you and fight for you.

He will go before you and subdue your enemies and give you victory. He is a man of war! If the enemies are trying to get you out, release a war cry right now! Declare war! Get in the Holy Ghost and begin to war! They think that you are alone. They think that you are unable to defend yourself. What they don't know is that your God is a God of war.

Throw your head back! Throw your head back and shout:

**Plead my cause, O God!**
**Plead my cause, O God!**
**Plead my cause, O God!** with them that strive with me: fight against them that fight against me.

David was not innocent, but he knew that he belonged to God. In Psalm 35, he cried out to God. He said, "Plead my cause, O Lord." I wonder if you know what it means to plead?

Have you ever stopped to think about 'A Plea'? Did you know that it is a legal terminology? A plea is a statement made in court by a person accused of a crime. A guilty plea means the defendant admits to all the charges and is ready to accept punishment.

A plea of not guilty means the defendant denies the charges. A plea bargain is when a defendant pleads guilty or no contest in exchange for a specific sentence.

A plea is an urgent or emotional request for help or mercy. In the court of law, you are asked, "What do you plea?" Well, believers do not plea guilty or not guilty. Neither do we make a plea bargain.

Instead, we plead the blood of Jesus Christ of Nazareth! When we do this, the blood of Jesus takes our wrongs and makes them right. That means the price has already been paid. That means we already have a Lawyer in the courtroom, and He is speaking on our behalf. Glory be to God!

So, David was calling God to take his case. David said, "I am not innocent, God, but if you are my Lawyer, you can speak on my behalf." Let us do it like David.

In the King James Version (KJV), he said,

*"Plead my cause, O Lord, with them that strive with me: fight against them that fight against me."*

In the Bible in Basic English (BBE), he said,

*"O Lord, be on my side against those who are judging me; be at war with those who make war against me."*

I wonder if you have anyone pointing fingers at you. Is anyone condemning you? Is there anyone saying that you are nothing or that you are no good? Every side you turn their fingers are pointing at you. I can relate! King David can, too. So, he took up his pen and wrote to his Lawyer.

In the Easy English Bible (EEB), he wrote, "Lord, please attack those people who are attacking me. Fight against those people who are fighting against me."- 'Plead' is derived from the Hebrew word 'rib'. It means 'to strive, to contend. For this reason, people sacrifice so much to retain the services of a lawyer with an excellent track record.

Can you relate to the plight of the Israelites? Their enemies were usually stronger and well-fortified than they were. Except in a few cases, they were also outnumbered. They were not trained for warfare and had no army in the early stages of their pilgrimage.

I do not know about you, but I have been up some rough mountains. I have been in some deep valleys. I have been surrounded before; armies behind me and before me billows roared as the Red Sea. But I learnt from my brother David, how to lift mine eyes to the hills.

Do you know who is there? The Source of my help dwells in those hills. That is where my help comes from. All of my help cometh from the Lord!

Where does your help come from? Is there anyone beside you? If there is, ask, where does your help come from? Well! Well! Well! Mine does not come from the prime minister, leader of the opposition, or member of parliament. It does not come from the president of the United States of America, Canada, or the King of England. All of my help cometh from the Lord!

He is a man of war! He has never lost a battle! I am here to let you know that you can depend on Him because He never fails. Come on and give Him your best praise.

He has never lost a case in the courtroom. He has never failed in the classroom. He never fails in the examination room. He has never misdiagnosed an illness or conducted a faulty surgery in the operating room.

My God can be trusted! He never fails! My daughter Shamowyah, testified on her birthday how faithful God has been to her over the years. A portion of her testimony has never left my mind since.

She reminisced on her academic journey from when she was eleven years of age. She recalled being in the second stream, which was for slow learners at the most prominent primary school in the parish of Westmoreland.

She was not positioned to be successful in the national examination being administered at the time - the Grade Six Achievement Test (GSAT). She could not read or write at this age.

Many negative words were released regarding her future in the academic world, especially by some teachers. She was distraught and came crying. The Lord brought a missionary into the ministry who operated a private academic institution. I approached her with my daughter's case and she agreed to assist her.

I took my little girl, placed my hand on her head, and asked her which school she wanted to attend. She said, "Daddy, I want to go to Hampton." Now, this is one of the most prestigious high schools for girls in th e island of Jamaica. I came in agreement with her because I know my God and I prayed over her. I said to my daughter, "Whatever you ask God today, He is going to grant it."

Glory be to God! Guess what? In less than one year, my daughter could read and write. Not only that; she was placed in the top tier of students who passed for Hampton that year.

The enemy began to release negative words over her life once again. This time, the attacks came from some church people who were ignorant of God's power to work these kinds of miracles. Some said Shamowyah would not complete Hampton because she was placed there by favouritism, and others said it was the principal of the Preparatory school from which she graduated who 'pulled strings' for her.

I laid my hands on her head another time and said to her, "Don't worry! God is fixing you, my baby!" The faithful God that I serve put them to shame again.

She went through the first five years of Hampton with flying colours; receiving a silver award at every grade. Silver and gold awards were given to students who excelled at each grade level. It did not stop there; she was successful in all her CXC's and went on to sixth form.

She passed all her CAPE subjects and received a gold award in her final year at Hampton. Shamoywah will complete her final year of study at the University of the West Indies - in Two Thousand and Twenty-Five – the year of Great Grace!

I did not share her testimony to try to convince anyone that she is brilliant or smarter than others. Instead, I wanted to join her in testifying of the Great Grace that sits upon her and that is resting on me.

Recently, I shared this with those travelling to and from Kingston with me. I told them that I am not an excellent driver. My skills are not what get us through the hundreds of miles on the King's business weekly. I said, do not get it twisted! It is only possible because of the great grace of God that sits on me and takes me to and fro!

If you can relate, let somebody know that He is in my classroom. He is in my courtroom. He is in my operating theatre. Open your mouth and praise Him, if you have that confidence of His omnipresence.

I know that some of you lack that confidence, either because you do not yet have a relationship with Him or because even as a Christian, you have not truly put your trust in God. It is not too late to get Him in your room.

Stop what you are doing and call Jesus in your room. Call Him in your room! This message might sound simple to you, but I will let you know that it is the best message that you will ever hear. If Jesus comes into your room to dwell, everything in your life shifts.

Did you hear what I just said? If God comes into your room, your situation, or your life, things can never remain the same. If He shows up at your Red Sea, if He becomes your man of war, you will never lose another battle. That is what I need to let you know before this book closes.

Say: Plead my cause O Lord! Plead my cause O God! Fight against them that fight against me!

Some of you are under pressure. I do not know what is fighting you. I do not know who is fighting you. But this I can say assuredly, whatever or whoever is fighting you, you cannot defeat the God who sits in heaven.

If you ever get Him on your side and He steps into your situation to plead your cause, all your enemies have to pack up, back up, back down or get thrown down and destroyed.

If you ever intreat God, and He steps forward to fight for you today, my God from Zion! That thing or that one cannot win! I know that sometimes their looks are intimidating. Judging from your appearance, they assume that you have no 'backitive' - support system. You appear to be alone, weak, feeble, and helpless.

They stare at you with scorn as if you are nobody. You become the ideal prey for them. They soon launch their attacks, especially with words and unclean spirits. But I am not intimidated by any witch, wizard, sorcerer, obeah worker, manager, supervisor, or any devil fighting you at this moment in your life. Your help is here!

With the knowledge you now have, you are not going to sit there and let them kill you. You are not going to lay there helpless and allow them to eat you alive and destroy your little flesh anymore. You are getting up today.

Regardless of whatever or whoever is fighting you, you are going to get up, open your mouth, and call on God for help right now. This is not the time to play cute. Come on warrior, you can do it!

You may wonder why I say you should open your mouth. Well, those to whom I minister often hear me say that a closed mouth cannot be fed. If you need a visitation from God, you must be willing to make your input.

Open your mouth and ask God today for divine intervention. You will never collect the spoils in this hour, unless God fights these enemies for you.

Come on now! Pray this intercessory prayer aloud. Get in the Holy Ghost and petition the throne of God. Do not stop crying until there is a shift in your situation. Come on!

This is personal because each person has their own battle. Even in a marriage relationship, when you place your heads on the pillow and go to sleep, the attacks will be different. You won't likely be engaged in the same warfare in the night watches. So, get radical and get personal with this moment of intercession.

Zoom in on your personal battles. I know that some persons are dealing with some real serious situations. Some of you are surrounded by some high-ranking demons, devils, witches, wizards and warlocks.

Some persons are dealing with poverty battles. Others are faced with battles of oppression, suppression, and depression. For some, the battle is addiction.

What is your battle? It is time to zoom in on your battles. Lift your right hand.

Prayer

Father, please begin to speak to your people's minds. Reveal to them the battles they are fighting, so that they can give it back to you.

Please, Holy Spirit, give victory to your people as they intercede now, in Jesus' name. Amen

Now, position yourself where eavesdropping spirits cannot hear your prayer. If you cannot find a closet, place your hand over your mouth when you are going to mention any personal information. We are going in and we won't stop until there is a breakthrough.

Call your battles by name and then ask God to fight those battles for you. Some battles are caused by demons of hate. There are also generational curses and battles within bloodlines. There are battles among family members and battles in the bedroom. Whatever it is, call it as you go before God.

Use this intercessory prayer for your situation. It is good to pray for others, but right now, focus on yourself. If you are not facing anything, go ahead and stand in the gap for someone you know is under attack.

Be sure to cover yourself and your loved ones under the blood of Jesus before you begin to pray. You can also anoint yourself with consecrated olive oil, as you are led by the Holy Spirit. Are you ready?

## Intercessory Prayer for God to defeat your enemies

*Lord! Mighty man of war! Strive with them that strive with me. Fight against them that are fighting against me. Fight them God! Fight them God! Fight them Holy Ghost!*

*Arise Holy Ghost! Lord dispatch warring angels to fight for me. I can't manage them God. I am outnumbered Lord! Please Jesus, fight! Fight! Fight them, Lord; until they are no more.*

*Arise! Arise! Arise O Lord! Fight them O Lord! All the secret haters! All the secret hypocrites! All those who are conspiring against me to destroy my flesh. Turn them against each other Lord.*

*I don't know them Lord but you know them. They are hiding in secret and plotting against me without cause. Expose and destroy them Lord. O God! You have seen their relentlessness. If you do not intervene, they are going to destroy my life.*

*Lord, they want me to backslide. They want me to leave the church. O my God, they are conspiring to get me fired from the job. Father, their evil altars are not hidden from Your eyes God. Help! Help! Help Lord! They are using evil words and witchcraft to destroy my family. My business and ministry are on their hit list.*

*God, you have heard their evil prayers. Plead my cause O Lord! Help! I look to You mighty man of war. I cry out to you Lion of Judah. O Lord, come and do what only You can do, Jesus.*

*O, let me not be ashamed! Let not my enemies triumph over me, Lord. Hear my cry O God! Hear my cry for help. I am desperate my God. Do not let them laugh O God. My trust is in You and You alone.*

*I can't manage them God, but You can manage them. Fight my battles O God! Fight it! Fight it! Fight it Jesus.*

*That which is fighting my children, fight it Lord. Lord that which is fighting against my.*

*(name your situation) Fight it Holy Ghost!*

*Take hold of shield and buckler Jesus. Guard my heart O Lord.*

*Let me not get bitter; let me not become hateful. Guard my heart O God, let me not seek revenge.*

*Lord let me not engage in physical warfare. Lord let me not lose faith in Your power to give me victory in these battles. Put on me the breastplate of righteousness. Please protect my heart O Lord.*

*Keep my heart and mind stayed on You as I wait on You to show up in this situation. Keep me in perfect peace. Keep my mouth with a bit and a bridle, while the enemies are before me.*

*Teach me how to love and pray for my enemies, because the battle is Yours and not mine. Teach me how to stand still and see Your salvation in my troubles, O God.*

*Release Great Grace on my life now O Lord, that I can smile amid this turmoil. Raise me up so that I can praise you while I am going through my storm.*

*Lord, in the end, I will testify of Your mighty works as I collect the spoils; when You have utterly destroyed my enemies.*

*Father, I praise You!*

*Lord, I thank You!*

*Hallelujah!*

*Hallelujah!*

*Glory to God!*

*Thank You Jesus!*

Now, Jehoshaphat told the people that there were two pre-requisites to living a victorious life of affluence and influence. The first is to believe in the Lord God to be established. The second is to believe in His prophets so that they can prosper.

It has been a very humbling experience, but I have been and will continue, by God's great grace, to be His mouthpiece. And I release over your life the word He gave me for this hour. 2025 is 5 O'clock in the realm of the spirit. It is: The Hour of Great Grace and Collecting of the Spoils. What time is it?

It is time to get back what the enemies have stolen. It is time to watch God defeat your greatest enemies. It is time to collect the spoils from the enemies that God has destroyed forever from your life. Do not allow unbelief to hinder you.

Receive your healing!
Take your deliverance!
Get that breakthrough!
Glide in great grace!
Collect the spoils!
If not now, when? If not you, who?

It's 5 O'clock! Go get what is yours in Jesus' name. Reap the end-time harvest as the kingdom of God continues to advance forcefully.

Welcome to the eleventh hour of the day!

# About the Author

Apostle Winston George Baker was born and raised in Savanna-La- Mar, Westmoreland, and has fathered six beautiful children.

He accepted Jesus Christ as his Lord and Saviour at the Holiness Born Again Apostolic Church in Savanna-La-Mar, on October 6, 1996.

Apostle Baker was ordained Pastor in 2006, Elder in 2009, and was installed as Bishop in 2011 at the Word of Wisdom Apostolic Church.

Apostle Baker is a man of profound faith and wisdom, a great leader and teacher whose life is epitomized by the Word.

On October 26, 2012, Apostle Baker founded the King Jesus Pentecostal Fellowship Church, which has now expanded to nineteen branches - seven locally and twelve internationally. They are as follows:

| Locally | | Internationally | |
|---|---|---|---|
| Kingston | 2 | United Kingdom | 4 |
| St. Elizabeth | 1 | USA | 4 |
| Westmoreland | 3 | Canada | 2 |
| St James | 1 | Cayman Islands | 2 |

From the outset of his ministry, Apostle Baker's passion for the kingdom was evident. The Lord has been faithful to his Word, and thousands of souls have been added to the church and were baptized in the name of Jesus Christ.

This man of God has the anointing of the Lord heavily upon his life. He has been used by the Lord over the years to heal the bodies from diverse infirmities such as HIV, cancer, diabetes, hypertension, fibroids, and kidney disease. The sight of the blind has been restored, the ear of the deaf open, demons cast out, babies talking to the Apostle from the womb, and even the dead brought back to life.

Still, Apostle remains humble, knowing that the miracles, signs and wonders, that the Lord has used him to manifest on the Earth, are all for God's Glory.

Under the mantle of the Great Commission, found in **Mark 16:15**, Apostle has carried the Gospel of Jesus Christ to the Cayman Islands, Turks and Caicos, United States of America, Israel, Bahamas, St. Maarten, Antigua, the United Kingdom and across the island of Jamaica.

Apostle Baker was inspired by the Lord to so far author four dynamic books namely: "*Warring Unclean Spirits* "(2016), *The Leader Who Covers* (2017), "*The Kingdom Mandate*" (2019), "*From the Guttermost to the Uttermost*" (2023) and his current book "*Its 5'O Clock – The Hour of Great Grace and Collecting the Spoils*". He was also inspired to write other books, which will be coming soon.

Apostle Baker's services are streamed on various media platforms, including Facebook, YouTube, Tik Tok, King Jesus TV and Vibes Radio Station of which he is the owner.

Additionally, you may shop at his online store, "Winston Royal" at

www.winstonroyalinternational.com

Apostle firmly believes that one should study the Word of God and that through fasting and an active prayer life, one can develop a relationship with God. He believes victory is inevitable for those who trust in God and that God can turn around one's life in twenty-four hours.

To God be all the glory.